AUNT JANET'S
LEGACY TO HER NIECES.

MRS BATHGATE.

AUNT JANET'S
LEGACY TO HER NIECES

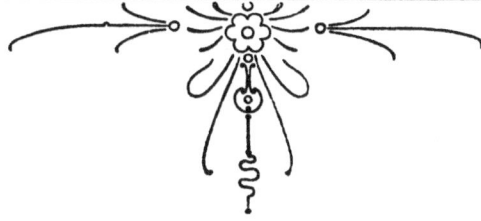

RECOLLECTIONS OF
HUMBLE LIFE IN
YARROW IN THE
BEGINNING OF THE CENTURY

. BY .

MRS JANET BATHGATE

SELKIRK
GEORGE LEWIS & SON

MDCCCXCIV

PREFACE TO FIRST EDITION.

THE Author of these Recollections had no thought while writing them of their appearing in any other form than in manuscript, or being read outside the circle of her own relatives and friends, to whom she thought they might be interesting and helpful.

"Aunt Janet" can now look back over a life of fourscore years and more. She was taught in her earliest youth to fear God, and all along she has been impressed with the feeling that His beneficent power is over all. She hoped to communicate this sense of the ever present guiding hand of a Father to her young friends, so that when similar trials and difficulties to hers meet them in the battle of life, they may look to the same source for strength and comfort.

The story is a record of the common every-day events of a life begun eighty years ago in the quiet pastoral valley of the Yarrow. Many changes have occurred since then. The world has made much progress in discovery and education, but, reader, with the advance of civilisation, does it not seem true that the love of many is growing cold, that we are in danger of losing the simple faith of our fathers? Perhaps this story may recall to your mind the simplicity and trust of your own early youth, and help you to realise where you now stand. Perhaps it may bring to mind stirring events long forgotten, when God's goodness was borne in upon you. If so, its publication, kindly insisted upon by her Nieces, will more than carry out the original intention, as it will greatly rejoice the heart of "Aunt Janet."

PREFACE TO SECOND EDITION.

THE Author of these Recollections was not more surprised that they ever appeared in the shape of a book than she has been at its acceptance by the public, the whole of the first edition having been sold within a year. And now that a second edition is called for, the Author looks up to God for His blessing on every reader who may derive any spiritual help from its pages. And may thanks be rendered to God, from whom cometh down every good and perfect gift. All good must descend before it can ascend.

The Author only claims, according to any light she sees in God's light, to serve Him with His own in any way He thinks fit to use her. And to the Father and the Son and the Holy Spirit be all the glory!

As many friends who have read the little book have pressed the Author to write a second volume, to all such she would say that it would have been a great pleasure to have recorded all the way in which God has led her through this great and terrible wilderness, in which none of His promises have failed. But to go back sixty years, and recount the incidents and events of a very checkered life, would, at her advanced age, be work for which she is utterly incapable. Let it suffice for her to record that goodness and mercy have followed her all the days of her life, and to-day, in the beginning of 1894, in her eighty-eighth year, her cup overflows.

CONTENTS.

———

ILLUSTRATIONS.

Aunt Janet's Legacy to her Nieces.

I.

The Flitting.

ANET GREENFIELD was born of poor but pious parents early in the century at Sunderland, a little hamlet two miles from Selkirk, and on the old road to Edinburgh by Yair Bridge. While she was yet an infant her father removed to Philiphaugh farm, on the opposite side of the valley from the old burgh, the capital of the Forest country. The farm-house then stood on the spot now occupied by Philipburn. Philiphaugh was then, as it is now, a beautiful place, backed with hills covered with heather, and surrounded by glens and roads well wooded, and near at hand was the Lang-rigg, under which sleeps the precious dust of some hundreds of Covenanters who fell at the battle of Philiphaugh.

It is here where we make our acquaintance with little Jenny, who is now in her seventh year. It is Whitsunday term, and a lovely May morning. The family is about to remove to a considerable distance up the Yarrow, and all is bustle and hurry. Even on this flitting morning family worship is not forgotten, and breakfast being over, the work of removing the furniture and getting it packed is begun. The box beds are taken down; and rosy-cheeked boys of the family, delighted to see one article after another removed, vie with each other in regaining long-lost treasures, in the shape of balls, bools, and peeries.

Little Jenny is sitting in a corner, quiet and rather sad looking, with pussy in her lap. Two carts are already loaded with the furniture, and have taken the road; the third, with sacks stuffed with straw, is ready to carry the members of the household. The children are in a hurry to be seated, the boys taking their places near their father, who is the driver on this great and exciting occasion, whilst the girls nestle round their mother; and the cart moves on.

The neighbours accompany them to the bridge across the burn, their lamentings and regrets mingling with the clamour of the other children of the place, and suggesting that the departing family had been well liked. The cart halts as it has reached the bridge, kind words are uttered, and the farewells are spoken. At this point the mother's eye is turned towards her offspring; she counts five of them, but where is the sixth? little Jenny is wanting. The mother gets out of the cart, heedless of the astonished throng, and makes for the empty house. She calls, " Jenny, Jenny!" but there is no answer. Into the neighbours' houses she goes, but with no better result; then she turns round the house into the kailyard.

In a corner of the ground, between the house and a wall that encloses the yard, is a little flower garden, which had been fondly tended by Jenny and her brothers. Did I say a flower garden? There was not the variety of flowers then that there is now, and you will perhaps smile when I tell you that a few daisies, marigolds, and a few roots of peppermint and southern-wood composed almost the whole stock, but to Jenny they had become part of herself. Here she stands, her eyes resembling the blue-bells of her native land bathed in the morning dew, for she was in tears at the thought of parting with her treasures; her rosy cheeks and red lips are made more bright by the briny streams that are making their way over them; her chestnut locks fall in careless profusion over her shoulders. Thus she stands in drugget frock and white pinafore; her bare feet just washed clean for the last time in the little burn where she and her brothers had so often "paidled," and to which on this morning they are bidding a long farewell. The mother in her gladness takes hold of Jenny, yet cannot help chiding her.

" Lassie, what do you mean?" she says; "the cart is stannin' ready to go, and your father is angry." But Jenny still clings to the daisies which she had been trying to root up, saying, " Mother, can we no tak' them wi' us?"

" No, no, bairn; they would soon wither. Stupid thing, dry your tears. My lassie, if you leeve lang you will get more to do with them."

Yes, good woman, your prophecies shall be fulfilled; your little Jenny shall have glimpses of sunshine, but her sorrows shall also abound. We must not, however, anticipate. For the present, Jenny's tears are wiped away by the hand of the fond mother—a silent act which in the future will help her to put her trust in Him whose love transcends that of the tenderest earthly friend; for

> What a tender hand is His
> That clothes the lilies fair,
> And o'er the meanest thing in life
> Takes more than mother's care.

Jenny is lifted into the cart and seated by her mother's side; pussy is placed in her lap, and her father remarks, "She will dae noo, she has a bit tender heart, and canna dae withoot something to show her liking for." Her mother, notwithstanding her hurry, had herself plucked a daisy in the garden, and now places it in Jenny's bosom.

The cart moves on, and their way is along the road which skirts the battlefield. In a little while they come in sight of the Yarrow. The General's Brig is passed, and Harehead is reached, near which Montrose's army was finally defeated. The scene recalls to the memory of the parents the tales of the Covenanters, their sufferings, and cruel deaths; and their own troubles feel lighter; for in spite of themselves they had felt somewhat sad on this May morning. The boys recite portions of the old ballad—

> " On Philiphaugh the fray began,
> At Harehead wood it ended,
> The Scots out o'er the Graemes they ran ;
> Sae merrily they bended."

And the girls sing—

> The widows did weep and the maidens did say,
> Why tarries my lover ?
> The battle is over,
> Is there none left to tell us the fates of the day ?

Then they all join in the old ballad, " The Flowers o' the Forest."

Now they are fairly on the banks of the Yarrow, and its gentle murmur and the singing of birds are almost the only sounds that were heard. Little Jenny, hitherto, had been saying little. She had been thinking more than she had been uttering ; her heart had been going backwards to the scenes and the companions she had just left, and she now breaks silence by saying, " Mother, who is going to live in our house now ? "

" Bairn," the mother says, " the house was not ours ; there is one building for us at Dryhope, where we're going to ; Dryhope is a bonnie place on the side of St Mary's Loch, which many a one has come far to see."

" But, mother, are there hills and heather bells and crawberries at Dryhope ? and is there a Corbie Linn ? "

" Hills, bairn ! plenty o' hills and burns—Dryhope burn and Kirkstead burn—and there's the Wardlaw, a beautiful green hill just at our door."

" And, mother, when I'm big I'll gang to service and get a big wage, and I'll buy our ain house and kailyaird, and we'll a' gang back again to Philiphaugh."

"Yes, yes, Jenny, you will do that, I daresay; but see, gi'e pussy a drap milk oot o' the bottle."

"Gudewife," said her husband, "gar Jenny haud her tongue, and put a' that nonsense out o' her head. One would think, to hear her speak, that she had as gude a richt to Philiphaugh as the Outlaw Murray, when he said to the king, 'Philiphaugh is mine by richt.'"

"Na, na, gudeman, you and me in our day built juist sic' like castles in the air oorsel's; and hers like ours will one day fall o' their ain accord."

"Weel, I daursay ye're richt, gudewife; the Book says 'sufficient to the day is the evil thereof.' Our little Jenny is mair God's than ours. He will watch over her; we can trust Him."

Yes, good people; and your trust shall not be disappointed. He whose eyes are in every place, and takes in all the works of His hands, will watch over your little Janet. She shall revisit one day the scenes of her childhood, with difficulty identify the spot where her father's house had stood, and kiss the grass which covers the corner where her much loved flowers grew long ago. But long ere that your kind hearts will have ceased to beat, and your eyes be sealed in their last repose. Sorrow they shall no more see; but in so far as you have glorified God, and are worthy to be numbered among the righteous, you will be had in everlasting remembrance. By that time the lustre will have faded from the blue eyes of your little Jenny, and her once rosy cheeks will be furrowed by the salt tears that shall meanwhile find their way over them; her locks will have grown like the snow, but her heart have lost none of its warmth. For she will find a satisfying portion in Him who is altogether lovely; her heart will be filled with joy, though her name will be no longer Jenny, but Naomi.

To return to our story. The cart, with its precious load of young and old, is now approaching the hamlet of Yarrowford. At the far end of the row of cottages, near to the gate that leads to The Hangingshaw, is a little thatched house. There we see a little old woman standing at the door, wearing a snow white cap, a wincey gown, and a blue and white checked apron; and she looks along the road as if expecting some one.

"Who can she be?" said Jenny's mother. "She is surely coming to meet us. I believe it's Elspeth Laidlaw; ye maun stop the cairt, John, and let us speir hoo she is."

"Nae doot Elspeth is coming to gi'e us her blessing, and we will baith be the better for hearing it," said John. "Hallo! Elspeth, is this you? How are ye this morning?"

"Blessed be God who has led me to grey hairs, I am weel; a pilgrim on this earth as all our fathers were, John; though I'm no sae like it as you and yours this morning."

"O! Elspeth," returned John, "I'm maybe takin' a wrang step, and it looks as if the road was getting darker. I'm gaun up tae Dryhope, far frae the kirk, and far frae the schule, wi' a' thae bairns." And the good man put his hand to his brow to hide the tears that were ready to flow from his eyes.

"Hout, John, man," said his aged friend, "dinna be cast doon; mony a yin's near the kirk and far frae God, and some that are far frae the kirk are near to Him. And though the Lord be so great that the heaven of heavens cannot contain Him, He is so kind that he delights to dwell with him that is of a contrite heart and trembles at His word. And as for your bairns, John, you maun juist dae like Abraham—teach them yoursel', for I'm thinking that there were naither schules nor kirks in his day, gude man; but the Lord said, ' I know Abraham that he will command his children and his household after him.' But let Tibbie and the bairns oot, and tie the horse tae the yett, and gi'e it a pickle o' the cow's hay; and come in and comfort your hearts wi' a morsel o' meat, and then gang on your way rejoicing in the Lord."

"O! Elspeth," says Tibbie, "ye *are* kind; and it's true that 'as iron sharpeneth iron, so a man sharpeneth the countenance of his friend.' As truly as God sent His angels to meet Jacob in his trouble, He has sent you to cast the oil of love on our troubled waters this day, and we are comforted."

While John is attending to the horse, Elspeth sets out the dinner; wooden trenchers and horn spoons grace the table, and kail[1] and pease-bannocks are the simple, wholesome fare.

"Elspeth," says Tibbie, "I fear that you have not only put yoursel' tae a lot o' trouble on oor accoont, but also tae expense."

"Na, na, Tibbie, dinna think aboot that. I never

[1] Scotch broth.

SELKIRK FROM PHILIPHAUGH IN 1850.

gang beyond what the Lord gi'es me. I asked Robin Hogg, the carrier, tae bring me a sheep-heid and trotters frae Selkirk, so I juist hung on the kail pot, and put a sprinklin' o' barley, and a bit leek, and twae three young nettles; for, ye see, oor greens are a' dune, and though it is maybe no the finest fare, it's better than oor forefaithers had, whan they were hunted like paitricks amang the hills and glens, and there read and prayed at the risk o' their lives. So, ye see we're rale weel off; and let us be thankfu'."

The bairns are now arranged round the table. The father gives a tender look, all eyes are closed, their hands are lifted up, as their wont is; and he pours forth his thanksgiving to the Giver of all good, for spreading a table in the wilderness, and also for the refreshing waters of kindness that have bubbled up from the well of the widow's heart. Having done justice to the pease-bannocks and nettle-kail, Elspeth presses them to have a little more; but all are satisfied.

"Hoo gled I am," says the good woman, "that there's still some left, for if ye had ta'en a' I would ha thocht that there hadna been eneuch; but blessed be His holy name, He never maks mooths but He gi'es something to fill them. And now, John, let us return thanks to Him who filleth the hungry and satisfieth the wants of every living thing. Let us no be like some in oor day, who juist say twae or three words when they begin, juist as if it were tae please Him. Na, na, let us not only thank Him for the bread that perishes, but also for the

Bread of Life that cometh down from heaven for the life of the world. May we evermore eat this Bread; and let Him kiss us with the kisses of his mouth, for His love is better than wine."

The good man opens his mouth, and out of the fulness of a grateful heart thanks God for all His goodness and mercies, and closes with a prayer that, as in days gone by, He that is unchangeable in wisdom, and power, and goodness—the Almighty Father of the spirits of all flesh, who fainteth not, neither is weary—might be pleased to increase the widow's handful of meal and her cruse of oil."

But like all other days, this one is hurrying on, and however sweet it is to recount all the way in which God has led us—levelling down the mountains, filling up the valleys, making the crooked straight and the rough places plain, leading the blind by a way that they know not—the friends must part, but in the assured hope that one day they will reach the haven of rest. However pleasant it would be to linger over this scene by the way, we must pursue our story.

The travelling family are all again seated in the cart. Elspeth lifts up her hands to the heavens, as if to remind them of God's watchful eye, saying, "Fear not to go down to Egypt, for I will go down with you and bring you up again."

"Amen," said John; and Tibbie added "If Thy presence go not with us, carry us not up hence."

As the farewells are spoken, tears are ready to flow; for they, the aged three, have a presentiment that the next time they meet, it may be by another river than the Yarrow, even the river of life, where all tears shall be wiped away, and their sun shall no more go down; for the days of their mourning shall be ended.

"Now, bairns, sit doon an' be quiet, said the father, an' dinna tease your mother wi' questions aboot this and that;" and giving the horse a gentle touch of the whip, he said, "Auld Bessie maun quicken her pace, or it will be late afore we get tae Dryhope at this rate."

Ere long they have arrived at the 'Dowie Dens o' Yarrow;' and John, addressing his wife, says, "Cheer up, guidwife; there have been some here in the days of langsyne that had deeper sorrow than ours;" and then he sings—

"Busk ye, busk ye, my bonnie bride,
    Busk ye, busk ye, my winsome marrow,
Busk ye, busk ye, my bonnie bride,
    And think nae mair on the braes o' Yarrow."

This proves a lullaby to little Jenny, who had got wearied as the day went on. She laid her head in her mother's lap, and sleep, that kindly friend which has soothed thousands of aching heads and hearts, comes to her relief. Jenny dreams that she wanders through woods and over hills—now in a big town, where all is hurry and confusion—then by the river Tweed—and through gardens and amid flowers, but they have no charm for her. No, no, that is not her garden; these are not her flowers. Away, away, in her dreams Jenny wanders across the hills, till she sits by her own garden, and sees the flowers there all in bloom. Beside her stands a person of transcendent beauty, with a look of tender love, and a voice soft and calm like the summer breeze. He stretches forth His hand towards Jenny's flowers, saying—"Dear child, consider how they grow; Solomon in all his glory was not arrayed like one of these. His was put on, but these take their beauty from the sap within; so, dear child, open your heart to the love of God, who loves even you; return His love. This is the sap by which you will grow to outward loveliness; by which you will grow up like a tree planted in His garden, watered every morning with the dews of His love. Your leaf will be ever green, and when others fade you will bring forth fruit, even in old age." When Jenny awakes, she feels soothed, she cannot tell why, but she tells her mother her dream.

"My dear lassie," says her mother, "God is preparing your heart for the seed of His kingdom; yes, God gives rain and sunshine to nourish the little daisy, as it looks up to the heavens, as it were, to thank Him; and the pure white snowdrop, so modest, which hangs down its head as if it were ashamed to be arrayed like the saints in glory. Man looks on the outward appearance, but the Lord looks on the heart. Jenny, dear, try and mind what God says—'For the grass withereth and the flower fadeth, but the word of the Lord endureth for ever.'"

As Yarrow Kirk is passed, many questions are asked by the children about a place they have often heard of, and their curiosity is gratified and their questions answered by the parents as best they can. Douglas Burn is crossed, and the father tells the boys that when they read the history of Scotland, they will learn a great many adventures of the 'Black Douglas.' The remains of his castle stand about two miles up the burn, near to Blackhouse farm ; and there is a very rough road to it. He tells them of that holy man Boston, who wrote the 'Fourfold State,' that their mother is never wearied reading, and who was once nearly lost there in a snowstorm. He was leading his horse up that burn-side when he could not see his hand before him ; he just stood still every now and again and spoke to Him who rides upon the storm ; and He brought him to Blackhouse, where he and all the family rendered thanks and praise for the great mercy shown to him.

At length we are in sight of St Mary's Loch. The cart halts, so that the children may get a look at that lovely sheet of water, and a marvellous sight it was to them, who had never seen the sea. The boys wonder if there are whales in it, at any rate there must be plenty trouts, and they will gump some of them some day. Oh ! the fun they will have !

II.

New Experiences.

JOHN GREENFIELD and his family reach their destination, and they stop at a low, old thatched house, wearied and hungry, and not a little disappointed that the new cottage they were to go into is not finished. This old house had been built with stone and turf, and the couples supporting the roof rested on the floor. There was only one window, with one pane of glass in it; no loft or upper apartment; there was a hole in the centre of the roof, through which the peat-reek had some difficulty in making its way; the earthen floor was uneven, and the place had a close and offensive smell.

Poor Tibbie's heart failed her at the sight of the miserable-looking quarters, for though she had never been accustomed to more than ordinary comfort, it was her pride and ambition to have her house clean and tidy. She had never been in such a place as this, and she says, "O! John, we can never gang into that house; we had better lie ootbye (outside); for every corner of the place is blacker than another."

Alas! what is to be done? All the out-houses and barns about the farm-steading are under repairs, for a new tenant had just taken possession. Mr Milne, the farmer, was a kind-hearted man, and he is at a loss to know what to do with the family till the new cottage is ready. At last the smearing-house[1] is fixed on, a house twice as long as it is broad. There is a bole[2] in one end, and a door, in two halves, in the other; and there is a strong smell of tar and wool in the place; but this latter is not such a drawback to Tibbie as it would have been to many others, for her father had been a shepherd, and she had been somewhat accustomed to the same kind of odour. In a short while the house is swept clean; fine new straw is got, and shake-downs are made up for the night. And plenty of good porritch and milk is sent from the farm-house. Supper over, the mother cries in the bairns, and before going to bed she says to her husband,

"Let us raise our Ebenezer to the Lord, who has so graciously helped us hitherto."

Tibbie had called, but little Jenny did not appear with the other children, and is not to be found. At length she is got in the stackyard running after pussy, which, in the confusion of the new quarters, had made her escape; but the cat is too busy among

---

[1] The house in which the sheep were besmeared with tar, or other materials, on the approach of winter.

[2] A square opening in the wall.

the mice to heed her call.   At last all are gathered in, and John says,

"I never saw a lassie like that Jenny; she is always in some trouble or other."

"Yes, gudeman; and so will every one be who comes under the burden of others; dae ye no think it's the very nature of love to be a burden-bearer? I believe that the care of the cat lies as heavy on Jenny's heart as Jenny lies on ours.

"Aweel, gudewife, I'll no dispute it; for I have read somewhere that the Apostle John, who leaned on the bosom of Eternal Love, and there so learned love that he appeared to speak of little else, rescued a poor cat from some cruel boys that had tied it to a tree and intended to stone it to death, and the poor liberated creature followed the good man all his life.   Whether the story be true or not, there is nothing in it contrary to the fine spirit of him who wrote, 'Little children, love one another, for God is love, and he that dwelleth in love dwelleth in God.'"

"Father," says Jenny, "will God take care of pussy?"

"Yes, yes, Jenny; now dinna greet, for it is written in the Psalms:

> Lord, Thou preservest man and beast,
> How precious is Thy grace,
> Therefore in shadow of Thy wings
> Men's sons their trust shall place.

Now, Tibbie, lock the door; and, bairns, compose yourselves, and let us sing to the praise of God the 23d Psalm, 'The Lord's my Shepherd.'"

All join in singing these sweet words to the tune " Martyrdom," and as they sing the closing lines—

> And in God's house for evermore
> My dwelling place shall be,

the thought arises, who would not like to be there !

"And now, bairns," says the father, "as this is a day much to be remembered by all of us, we'll go out of our regular reading ; let us read for our instruction the 90th Psalm, 'Lord, Thou hast been our dwelling-place in all generations.'"

When the reading was concluded, John said, with a kindly look, " Bairns, your notes." They were each accustomed to remember a little of the chapter read ; this commanded attention and strengthened their memories. Their father would be pleased with a single word, but it was felt to be a great short-coming to have nothing to say. Then all kneel down, and the father pours forth his confessions of sin, and thanksgivings for mercies past and for promises of strength for days to come. After concluding, the bairns are sent one by one to a corner —for there was no closet in the smearing-house—in which to say their prayers.

The father opens the door and goes out, as is his wont, for he has still some words to say that it is fit no ear should hear but His who is slow to wrath, forgiving iniquity, transgression, and sin. Some of the neighbours had been attracted by the singing, and are running away on his coming out. He hears them saying, " O, they are Cameronians ! Wattie

Laidlaw will get some of his ain kind noo—heepi-creets like himsel', nae doot."

On his return John tells Tibbie what he has heard, and she remarks, " How thankful we should be that there are some near us that fear God, and whatever the wicked ones think of them, the Lord knoweth them that are His."

To the labouring man rest is sweet, and they awake in the morning refreshed. Pussy has turned up, and Jenny ascribes it to God, as she tells her mother that she had prayed to God to send pussy back. Her mother replied, " And have you thanked your heavenly Father for His goodness ? " Jennie looked down, saying—

" Mother, I dinna ken very weel what to say. If I gang into a corner and say, ' Thank you, O God, for sending pussy back,' will He be pleased ? "

"Yes, yes, Jenny, He is even pleased with a grateful sigh. It is a comely thing to render thanks to God." Jenny ever after this went to God with her troubles, but she sometimes forgot, as others often do, to render thanks when deliverance came. It was well she had a Christian mother.

The boys had been early up, and had gone out to look round the new place. They met with some of the neighbours' boys, and got some information about the people around them. Willie came running in, saying, " Mother, here's a man they ca' auld Robin Laing coming with a barrowfu' o' peats; and, d'ye ken, Jock Swanston says he's just a miser. He keeps his door aye locked for fear o' ony body gaun in to steal his siller."

" Gae way, laddie, ye maunna believe a' ye hear ; it's no like a miser to be bringing us a barrowfu' o' peats."

" May I come in, guidwife ? " says Robin Laing. " I've brocht ye a wheen peats, for I'm thinkin' ye will need a fire this morning—that is, if ye ken where to put it."

" Come in, honest man ; and thanks to the Giver of all for putting it into your heart to show so much kindness to strangers, for I was not only at a loss where to put a fire, but at a loss where I was to get something to kindle it. So I'll just try it at the bole, and if the reek winna gang oot there, I'll try it at the door ; and I'm thankful that I have got something to kindle it with."

" Good woman, the Lord is a rich provider, and they that wait on Him shall not want. You are come here wi' a lairge faimily amang strangers, and I hope you know Him who is the strangers' shield."

" Yes, honest man, I know Him in part, and I am following on to know Him better ; and I take it as a proof of His faithfulness, that He has sent you this morning like a ministering angel. The peats were not more needed than your Christian sym-pathy, and in His mercy He has sent both."

" Alas, good woman, I have'na muckle to spare. It's forty years the-day since, like yoursel', I cam' wi' a lairge faimily to Dryhope, and since then I've had mony ups and doons, and now I'm left alane. They're no a' in the grave, but them that's alive are far away ; and I'm juist here wi' one foot in the grave—oh, dear me ! mair than one foot, for my

better half is there. I mean her dust, for my Peggy
got a wonderful glance o' the Saviour just afore she
set out to the land afar off, and I claim her still by
faith, believing that she is abune singing like a
laverock—but I'm forgettin' my errand: I may tell
you that my auld maister, Mr Ballantyne, has settled
a bit yearly income on me—the Lord bless and
reward him !—and he is gi'ein' me a bit hoose doon
at the Tinnis, and the cairts are comin' up to take
doon some o' the bits o' odds and ends that they could
nae tak' wi' them them the other day, and they are to
tak' me and my auld stuff with them when they
come up again; so I'll be away in the beginnin' o'
next week—that is, if the Lord should be pleased
to spare me—so I have a pickle peats that I no
need, and if ye would send the bairns to bring them
doon, they will haud ye in, maybe, till ye get yer ain
cuisen " (cast).

" Mony thanks, Robin ; the Lord loveth a cheerful
giver, and when He coonts up the cups o' water that
hae been gi'en in His name, He will no' forget your
kindness to us this day. I'm only sorry, Robin, that
you are leaving the place."

" Weel, gude woman, I must confess it is not without gey sair pangs in my auld heart that the last tie
to the dear place is to be broken ; but I am reconciled
to the Lord's will. You see there are twae sides
for everything : I'll be nearer the kirk, for ae thing ;
seeven miles back and forrit is abune my fit now-
adays. But the servant o' the Lord has paid me
mony a visit—that gude man, Mr Russell, I mean
—and though he is no' aye speakin' o' the Solemn

League and Covenant, like Wattie Laidlaw's minister, yet the love of God and man is always boilin' up in his heart, and the law of kindness is on his tongue. But I maun gang away, and let ye get on wi' yer wark."

" Weel, weel, Robin, God be with you; John and I will come up and gi'e ye a hand with the packing."

" O, dear me! how true the auld proverb, that 'gif-gaf mak's gude freends,' for I was just wonderin' whae I wad get to tak' doon the auld box beds. Jamie Morrey and Wattie Laidlaw, the gude, godly men, would willingly come; but I was loth to ask them, for they're workin' hard baith late and sune at the farm.

On the following evening, Tibbie and John pay Robin Laing their promised visit to help in packing the furniture. Robin's house looked cold and comfortless. The one he had formerly lived in had been blown down, and having been a dry-stone dyke builder, he had got leave from the late farmer to build a new house on the site of the old one; and it was of a very homely construction. The door was made of unplaned deals, and there was no plaster of any kind upon the walls; the fire was kindled upon the hearth-stone, which had not a grate upon it, whilst the furniture consisted of two box beds, a table, and a few other articles of necessary use. Though Robin was old and frail, yet there was no lack of sunshine in his face: his eyes bespoke a heart, not only at ease, but full of comfort and content. No lordly proprietor could have welcomed friends with more natural grace than he did his visitors.

"Come in, ye that fear the Lord, and be seated," he said. "I have a humble dwelling, but neither the stones nor the timber thereof shall rise up against me in the day of the Lord. No, if they could speak they would tell how many gracious visits I have had from Him who, while on earth, had nowhere to lay His head; and it would have been a sore heart to me this day if, while leaving this house, I had to leave Him behind me; but, blessed be His name, He has said, 'I will never leave thee nor forsake thee.'"

"So, Robin," said Tibbie, "you carry your treasure in your heart."

"Weel, gude woman, ye're partly richt, but I'm thinking my treasure carries me. My heart is in heaven; yes, God is the treasure of my soul," and, laying his hand on his bosom, Robin added, "He is also here."

"We're come to give you a bit hand wi' the packing up of the furniture," said John, "and if it be agreeable to you we might lock the door, and look up to Him for help who has brought us hitherto."

"As for the door," says Robin, "it's always locked, for ye see I was not able to get baith a sneck and a lock; and I am accustomed to turn the key when I come in, and then I feel that I am alane and can speak to Him undisturbed; so let us bow our knees, and lift up our hearts, with our hands, to God in the heavens, who is the hearer and answerer of prayer."

Robin and John pour out their hearts to God, and feel that He does not send them away empty. Then they go to work, and everything is put in order, to be lifted in the morning. They then part from each other, feeling in their sweet experience the truth of the Saviour's words, " Give, and it shall be given you, good measure, pressed down, and running over; for with what measure ye mete, it shall be measured to you again."

On their way home, Tibbie remarks, " How hard it is to be misunderstood by one's neighbours; for Robin, instead of having been in the habit of locking his door to count his guineas, as folk say, has done it to hold communion with his God."

" It is not strange, gudewife, that they should thus judge, whose gold is the only God they know. As for Robin, they may throw glaur at him, but it winna stick; Robin is without doubt the true gold purified in the furnace of affliction."

By the end of the week the families referred to had removed, as also had old Robin Laing, and now all on the farm are new hands—a wonderful change from the old state of things.

III.

With the Cameronians.

THE first week at Dryhope had been a busy one with Tibbie and the two elder girls, John lending a hand when he came in after the labour of the day. And on Saturday, the gudewife is deserving of much credit for her arrangements in the smearing-house. The box beds serve for a partition, so she has now " a-but-and-a-ben." The Sabbath morning finds them all well and comfortable, with hearts filled with thanksgiving and praise. The morning exercises are over, and John is just turning over in his mind Elspeth Laidlaw's advice to follow the example of Abraham. But he is at a loss where or how to begin. Well as he likes Dr Lawson as his minister, he is too wearied to think of going all the way of sixteen miles to Selkirk, and he has not yet made up his mind to go to Yarrow Kirk; though Dr Lawson said to him that he would get more good from Mr Russell than he would carry away. So he takes the Carritches[1] down from the shelf, and is about to get the children together, thinking he cannot do better than begin with them,

[1] The Shorter Catechism.

when a stranger makes for the door. He is a very pleasant-looking young man, and, coming into the house, he says—

"Gude morning, gude folk. I hope I am no disturbing you on this holy day of rest; my name is Wattie Laidlaw, I live down the burn-side there wi' Jamie Morrey. One of our ministers is to preach at Blackhouse the-day; so I just thought, as I was passing, and as ye're far from your ain kirk, that I would call in and tell you, as maybe some of you would like to gang and hear what the Lord has put into the mouth of His servant to say to us poor backsliding sinners; for we are not so hearty in the ways of the Lord as when they swore to the Covenants."

"Come in, Wattie," says John, "and take a seat till I throw on my coat. Tibbie, wumman, hand me doon my stick, and g'ie me oot my Sabbath-day hat—and, bairns! get ready, and we'll gang wi' a' our hearts to hear what the messenger of the Lord has to say. Though we dinna take the name of Cameronians, we claim kin to Christ, for whose name and kingship Cameron bled."

John, accompanied by the elder children, and Wattie, who volunteers to take charge of Jenny, make a group all alike happy and cheerful; for it would have been a long day in the smearing-house, learning from the Book of Proverbs, and they would have been like crows in a mist; for there was no window in it. The good man and his family are in their homespun clothes, from top to toe all of Tibbie's making, neat and clean. The neighbours

look at them as they pass, and say they are kind
o' gentry. John has coaxed Jock Swanston and
Wull Scott to accompany them. These were two
lads, from twelve to fourteen years; they wore
homespun blue plaiding coats with brass buttons,
and were bare-footed and bare-headed, with red
curly locks; fine healthy, open-faced lads they were,
but restless and wild-looking; and they every now
and again start a hare here and a rabbit there.
John's patience is nearly exhausted as he finds his
own boys would fain have joined in the chase, so
he halts to give them counsel.

"Now, laddies, you maun a' behave yoursel's;
we're going to worship the Lord God, who made
heaven and earth, and it becomes us to enter His
house with reverence."

Wull and Jock did not at all enter into the spirit
of the occasion, and with a hop-step-and-leap, and
a "hurrah for the Cameronians," they bound across
the moor for home.

"Let them gang," said Wattie, "they are reprobates, nae doot; let us be thankful that the Lord
knows His own elected ones."

In due time we arrive at Blackhouse, and reverently enter a considerable-sized kitchen. Nearly
in the centre is the fire-place; there is a long
chair on one side of it, and on the other are
seats of various shapes and sizes. The family of
the house, a few shepherds with their dogs, and
our company compose the congregation. The
minister, an elderly, serious-looking man, gives out
the first Psalm; after singing which, and prayer,

he takes his text from the second chapter of the Song of Solomon, third verse—"As the apple tree among the trees of the wood, so is my Beloved among the sons; I sat down under His shadow with great delight, and His fruit was sweet to my taste."

"Firstly," said the minister, "you will see this tree is a tree among many trees, but it has a special character; it is a fruit tree, but not a forbidden tree; a tree in its season, with foliage and fruit; under which the weary traveller through the dreary, thirsty desert finds a shadow and a shelter from the burning sun. So he sits down under its shadow with great delight. He not only finds there a cooling shelter, but he finds fruit; he does not look merely at its beauty, size, and form, but he eats of its fruit, and finds it sweet to his taste. Need I tell you, my brethren, that this tree represents the Son of God, who came down from heaven and took our nature. As a man, He walked among men, pure and holy, thus revealing the Father's idea for men—that they should live in love to God and one another; not in selfishness, and the love of money, which is the root of all evil. He says, 'Come unto me, all ye that labour and are heavy laden, and I will give you rest;' rest, by revealing the heart of your Father in heaven, whose love all your sins have not quenched, though His wrath is revealed against all sin; and He will never rest until He has destroyed it out of the universe. Yet He has no pleasure in the death of a sinner, but is ever saying, 'Why will ye die? Call Me thy

Father, and turn not away from Me.' Oh, dear brethren, have each of you learned to say truly, ' Our Father which art in heaven, hallowed be Thy Name?' If so, you are sitting under the shadow of the tree of life, and are finding His love sweet to your taste."

These are only a few broken recollections of this precious discourse, for the sermon was a long one; the whole service occupying two hours and a half. John had something to do to keep the boys from sleeping. Little Jenny had been drinking in more than she understood at the time, but having a retentive memory, what she heard became food for her in after days.

At the close, Wattie introduced his new acquaintance to the minister. The good man laid his hand on Jenny's head, and said, " You have been very attentive; you are a bonnie wee lassie; but never forget that favour is deceitful, and beauty is vain; but the woman that feareth the Lord she shall be praised."

On the way home Wattie and John talk much of what they have heard; and on arriving at the smearing-house, where everything is neat and clean, the table is spread for dinner, which consists of curds and pease-bannocks. Wattie is pressed to remain, and is not unwilling to do so, for he seems rather pleased with his new acquaintances, and they are glad of his company. A blessing is asked, and they all do justice to their humble meal; for, as the saying is, hunger is " good kitchen."

After dinner all are seated quietly, and the father

calls on the boys to tell their mother what of the sermon they can remember; but they appear nervously backward, and none of them answer—perhaps because of Watty's presence.

"Come on, John," says Tibbie, "you and Willie; and then Wattie will tell us what you dinna mind."

Willie says, "Weel, I dinna mind a word, because —because, faither, it wasna a kirk; it was juist a hoose, and the saits were a' splattered with suit[1] draps; and he was juist a man wi' a black toozie heid, and no' the least like Dr Lawson."

"O, Willie, ye maun learn that God is a spirit, and wherever He is worshipped in spirit and in truth, there is a kirk. Come, John, you will surely mind something."

"Weel, faither, I could hardly hear a word for yon dowg snorin'."

"O, bairns, bairns," said the father, "ye humble me this day before this good man, that came off his way to ask us to go with him to the House of God. Go away ben the hoose, and look ower the Proverbs, ye sluggards, and learn from the ant and be wise."

John and Wattie rehearse the sermon to Tibbie, and they find that the more they think of it, and speak about it, it grows the sweeter, and they confess that they have had a feast of fat things that day.

Father, accompanying Wattie down the burn-side a little way, cannot help expressing his fears lest his boys, coming in contact with wild lads, should learn their ways; and he is not a little comforted

---

[1] Soot.

to hear that the strange lads' families were expected to leave in the beginning of the week. Wattie remarks that an unrenewed heart is worse to get rid of than a bad neighbour.

" True, Wattie ; for God, that knows it better than we, says, it is 'deceitful above all things and desperately wicked;' but, blessed be His holy name, though He cannot mend an old heart He can give a new one, and we know that a broken and contrite heart for sin is well pleasing in His sight. Good night, Wattie; and God be with you."

" Good night, John, and the Lord bless you and yours."

So the friends part for the present, but they had many meetings and partings after that, and they never met nor parted without giving thanks to God for giving in each other a true brother. John has unexpectedly found a green spot in the wilderness, and he sings—

> Amidst scenes of confusion and creature complaints,
> How sweet to my soul is communion with saints.
> To know at the banquet of mercy there's room,
> And find in the presence of Jesus a home.
>> Home, home! sweet, sweet home ;
>> To find in the presence of Jesus a home.

> While here in the valley of conflict I stay,
> O give me submission and strength for my day ;
> Indulge me with patience to wait at Thy throne,
> And find even now a sweet foretaste of home.
>> Home, home! sweet, sweet home ;
>> To find in the presence of Jesus a home.

Lone St Mary's and its Churchyard.

WEEK after week passes by, the new house is often visited, and the kail-yard is turned over. Jenny gets a plant of southern-wood and some marigolds from Wattie Laidlaw. Dry-hope old tower, once the habitation of freebooters, is near by; and one day, Tibbie with her family visits St Mary's Churchyard. She had a special reason for going there. She had been for some years a servant at Eldinhope, some three miles down the Yarrow; and when the daughter of Mr and Mrs Scott, who were in the farm then, was married to Mr Gibson of The Glen, they were anxious that Tibbie should go to be a servant with her. She had gone to The Glen with the young wife; they had taken fondly to one another; and it was to see her grave that she went to St Mary's Churchyard that day. She is not long in finding there recorded on a tombstone, " To the memory of the beloved wife of T. Gibson of The Glen." She can read no more, but sits down, and amid showers of tears recalls the memory of days gone by, when the deceased and she took sweet counsel together and walked to the house of God in company.

The elder girls are moving about, but Jenny, as is her wont, keeps close by mother, and commits to memory, from her lips, the following lines inscribed on the headstone, which is still to be seen in the old burying-ground of St Mary's.

> She lived a humble, virtuous life,
> Shunned evil and wicked strife,
> Which gives good hope she is now above
> With Christ in everlasting love.

Tibbie and Jenny move on a little further, and find the two older girls and little Nelly much absorbed in looking at a large slab, on which they have tried in vain to make out the name of him whose precious dust lay underneath, and which the snows and rain and hail of many generations had almost blotted out. But they had now scraped the moss and the rust from the edge of the slab, and at last made out the following words—

The blessing of Him who was ready to perish came upon me, and I caused the widow's heart to sing for joy; I was eyes to the blind and feet to the lame, and a father to the poor, and the cause which I knew not I searched out.

Tibbie felt anxious to find out the name of one worthy of such a testimony, and what she learned from the tradition of the oldest inhabitant was as follows :—

His name was Thomas Linton, he lived at Chapelhope, and was an elder in Ettrick Kirk in the time of the Rev. Thomas Boston. In the days of persecution he suffered much, and lost all that he had. It was said of him that in those times he never locked his door, and that before retiring to rest he laid out on his kitchen table bread, butter, and cheese, so that the poor hunted sheep of the Good Shepherd might venture in and satisfy their hunger without being molested by any under his roof. It is said that he sometimes set down an old coat, a pair or two of stockings, and a shepherd's plaid. The meaning of their being so placed was well under-stood by those who were hiding in dens and caves of the mountains. Thomas Linton survived the persecution. He prospered greatly in worldly things and became very rich, but he was never married. He was a wise counsellor, a true comforter, and was sought after and looked up to by rich and poor in the place where God had cast his lot. This slab had been erected to his memory by his grateful neighbours, and the following lines were inscribed by his minister, Thomas Boston, of Ettrick :—

All lost for Christ a hundredfold produced; and he became a father's eye and feet unto the poor, the blind, the lame.

"So," said Tibbie, "the word of the Lord stands true. 'The righteous shall be in everlasting re-membrance.'"

Before leaving the locality Tibbie wishes to visit another traditional spot. A few yards from St Mary's kirkyard there is a square flagstone which is called Binnerim's Cross. Tradition says that he whose dust lies there was a Roman Catholic priest, who was proverbially cruel to the suffering flock of

Christ, hunting them out, and giving information to their enemies. This man was murdered—it was never known by whom—and according to the custom of those days he was buried where he fell; a smooth flagstone and a wooden cross marked the spot. For long the cross had disappeared, and the stone was nearly covered with moss. Tibbie, pointing to it, bids her bairns mark that while " the memory of the just is blessed, the name of the wicked shall rot." They now rejoin the boys, who had been bathing in the loch, and they got home weary and hungry; but all have had lessons of heavenly wisdom, which some of them would not forget to their dying day.

We feel this to be the fitting place to record another incident of the days spent beside St Mary's Loch. It is a fine summer morning. A gentle shower of rain had cleared away the mist, and the sun was, as it were, looking through tears, giving a soft refreshing calm to the heart of Tibbie and little Jenny as they go that morning to a field at the foot of the loch. They cannot tell how the wind bloweth nor where it listeth; they hear the sound thereof, but know not whence it cometh nor whither it goeth; but they shall yet know that that which comes from God leads to Him. Jenny and her mother have arrived at the field with the porridge, along with other cottagers on the same errand. It is nine o'clock. John calls to the workers, every hoe is thrown down; and all, alike hungry, do justice to the morning meal. They have scarcely finished, when every eye is turned upwards: a beautiful rainbow spans the heavens, and the calm waters of the loch reflect it as in a mirror. John starts to his feet, lifts off his hat, and calls to the workers—" Bairns, draw near, and let us worship the Lord who made heaven and earth, and set this bow in the cloud, spanning the heavens and reaching to the earth, as a token of His love and power." Then he bows his head reverently, saying " O Lord, Thy mercy is in the heavens, Thy truth is in the clouds; and in this symbol Thou art proclaiming Thy faithfulness to all generations. And we, a few of Thy erring children, lift up our waiting eyes to Thee, our Father which art in heaven: hallowed be Thy name, thy kingdom come, Thy will be done on earth as it is in heaven! Thou hast sworn by Thyself that the whole earth shall be filled with Thy glory. So let it be; and may it please Thee to fill every heart here with love, because Thou art lovely, and art faithful to all Thy promises."

" Now, bairns," he adds, " let us sing to His praise these refreshing words of one of the Psalms of David, the man after God's own heart—

> How excellent in all the earth,
>   Lord, our Lord is Thy name,
> Who hast Thy glory far advanced,
>   Above the starry frame.

So they all join and sing the whole psalm to a familiar tune. The song of the lark, the bleating of the lambs, the murmuring of the stream as it leaves the loch, make a befitting chorus, while John, Noah-like, standing with head uncovered, and a handful of out-door workers thus worship the Lord on the banks of the lonely Yarrow.

The road by which Jenny and her mother return that morning lies between two hedges, and every leaf and blade of grass was shining with pearly drops of dew; the spider in weaving his slender web had drawn his threads across the path from hedge to hedge. The beauty of the web attracted Jenny; she tried to lay hold on the airy threads, but they broke in her grasp, and she looked disappointed. Her mother observed her embarrassment, and remarked — "Jenny, dear, God in love to us, his thoughtless children, not only teaches us by the rainbow, but also by everything He has made. He is here teaching us that they who build their hopes on the things of this world, when death comes, they— that is the things of this world—will avoid their grasp just as the spider's web avoids yours. He says, "Love not the world, neither the things of the world;" like the spider's web they pass away, but they that fear to offend God, and trust in Him, when he makes a new heaven and a new earth, shall dwell in it for ever.

Pussy comes to meet them as they near the home; she fawns on Jenny, who halts and gives her a little milk out of the pitcher, and wonders if God will let pussy live on the new earth.

ʊ.

Knotty Points.

ENNY was a bright happy child naturally, but about this time she became very quiet and sad-looking. Her anxious mother thought her health was affected, but to all questions Jenny only answered, "I'm weel eneuch;" and so she felt in body, but her conscience was troubling her. She had one Sabbath, unobserved by her mother, slipped out her doll and played with it all the forenoon; but when night came, and she, along with her brothers and sisters, was, as usual, required to repeat the sentence of the righteous and of the wicked, she was awakened to a sense of her sinfulness in breaking the Sabbath. She felt that God had seen her wickedness and had written it in His great book; and her distress was very great. During the night she dreamed that she saw the heavens open, and an angel with a great book in his hand going forth throughout the whole world taking down the names of the righteous, and he was proclaiming aloud, "This is the Lamb's Book of Life." And Jenny asked him, saying, "Is my name in it?" and he answered "No."

At this Jenny awoke in great terror, crying that she was lost. Her mother found it difficult to persuade her that it was a dream, but something that her mother said about forgiveness gave her rest; for up to this time she did not know God's forgiving love.

"Jenny," said her mother, "pray to God to put you among the elected number."

"But, mother, what is the elected number?"

"Weel, Jenny, it is those that are elected that will be at God's right hand at the judgment day, and when once you are a good reader you will read that book you see me often reading, Boston's 'Fourfold State.' He explains all about election."

Jenny is puzzled and quite at a loss. But there is another whispering in her ear; she has not as yet learned his wiles, and she listens to his voice, which says—"You don't always run when your mother calls you, do you? No; sometimes you pretend that you don't hear her."

"Maybe, whiles," says Jenny to herself.

"Weel, then, why are ye so troubled about the judgment day? That's just when ye hear the last trumpet. Just you lie still in the grave, never let on ye hear it."

"Aweel," says Jenny, "that's grand—thank ye; I'm gled tae tak yer advice."

Then off flies the tempter, no doubt laughing in his sleeve; and it would have been well for Jenny if this had been the only time she had listened to the arch-fiend, who is ever going about "like a roaring lion, seeking whom he may devour." But there is One stronger than he, who will take him by the beard, and deliver the little lamb from his devouring jaws; and one day bruise his head, so that he shall deceive the nations no more for ever.

As soon as John had a quiet opportunity next day he said—

"Gudewife, what a rumpus was that that Jenny got up last nicht?"

Tibbie relates the circumstance, as it is given above, and very solemnly adds, "I believe, gudeman, that the Lord has gi'en oor bairn a special call. I'm quite sure she is one o' the elect."

"Aweel, gudewife, I hope ye're richt, but I heard ye telling her tae pray tae be put among the elect; but if she is elected from all eternity, as Boston says, her prayers are no needed on that score."

"But, gudeman, a praying person is Christian evidence; for, ye ken, reprobates canna pray."

"Aweel, aweel, gudewife, I ken that you and Boston were aye great freends, an' I dinna want ye tae cast oot, for I have aye been prophesying in my own mind aboot that bit lassie. Did ye no observe hoo earnest Dr Lawson prayed when he baptised her? And the Scripture says that "the effectual fervent prayer of a righteous man availeth much;" and whatever Boston was, there's naebody doots Mr Lawson's integrity. Oh, it warms my heart yet when I think hoo earnest he prayed that her name micht be recorded in the Book of Life; and another thing that has often struck me is that she is the very image of her great-grandmother,

Janet G——. A truer Christian woman than she was never lived. Only think of her and great-grandfather walking a' the way from Heriot to Midlem every Sabbath-day tae the Auld Licht Burgers, and this even when they were up in years; and I'm prood tae think that I have one o' the family named after her. I aye liked the name; yes, there's something in the name."

"But, gudeman, the lassie was called after her aunt at Selkirk."

"That's quite true, Tibbie; but her aunt was not the original, for I believe the seed of the righteous is blessed. Weel do I mind, though I was only eleven years auld, and my youngest brother was not born, when my father was killed by lichtnin'. I was standing beside him at the time, and, as I was going to say, weel do I mind my grandfather's prayer when he came in to comfort my mother, which was something like this:—'O our God, since it has pleased Thee to cut down the tree, we thank Thee that it has seemed good in Thy sovereign sight to spare the branches. Do Thou glorify Thy great name by throwing the lap of Thy cloak over this widow and her fatherless children; and grant that there may be a seed by us and by ours to serve Thee till the latest generation, even while the sun and moon endure.' So, gudewife, when I look on my bairns and remember this prayer, I take comfort; and though I love you and reverence Thomas Boston, yet I have more faith in prayer than in election; and I cannot help noticing Janet is as like her great-grandmother as can be. And did ye not observe how quickly Wattie

Laidlaw, the gude, godly man, picked her up, and how she clung to him yesterday. Ye may say what ye like, Tibbie, but it's a true saying that 'like draws to like.'"

"Weel, gudeman, if ye gang to that with it, what will ye make out of this? When she was just about a month old, when we were at Sunderland, and I had left her in the cradle, and left the door open, and gone out to milk the cow, Daft Jock Gray, of Selkirk, came in, and lifted her out o' the cradle, and ran off with her. Ye may think how my heart that day lap to my mouth when I missed her, and ran like one distracked to Jamie Pott, who was napping stones at the roadside, to ask him if he had seen onybody pass. So he told me that he saw Daft Jock come out o' our house carrying something. Jamie cast off his coat, and he ran, and I ran, and he owertook Jock at the Nettly Burn Plantin'; and the poor lamb was greetin', and the fiend slavering and kissing her. I aye thought Jock was mair rogue than fool, but he made the excuse that he was going to make a present of her to Dr Anderson of Selkirk, for cutting off his sore finger; for he had never paid him."

"Weel, gudewife, we should be thankfu' that it was na a lion that had come to devour her; and do ye no see it's just as I said, God watches over the seed of the righteous? He was teaching us a second time that she was His gift to you and me, that we might train her up in the fear of the Lord. But I maun just haud my tongue, for, Tibbie, ye maun aye ha'e the last word; but blessings on you, for you're a good wife and a kind mother."

We have seen how the evil one had calmed Jenny's conscience, as he has often done to older bairns than her; but the Word of God stands true, and it says, " Be sure, your sin will find you out." Some weeks passed by; Jenny had regained her rosy cheeks and cheerful happy way, but, alas! she observes that her mother is looking very ill and troubled.

It is Sabbath morning. One of the girls is sent to ask Anne Smail, Mr Milne's housekeeper, to come and speak with her mother; her father is hurriedly putting on his Sunday coat and hat, and a boy brings the master's riding horse to the door. When John is about to mount the horse, Tibbie says, " John, if Dr Anderson is not at home, just bring Clarkson."

Jenny also overhears her mother in a low voice giving her eldest daughter charges—" Nannie," she says, " you are to take Jenny and Nellie and Willie down to the farm-house to sleep there to-night till we hear what the doctor says; and, O bairn, if onything ails me, try and comfort your faither and be kind to the bairns."

Jenny is more than puzzled; she cannot speak. With the others, she is hurried away. She lies long awake that night. Is her mother going to die? If so, Jenny will die with her; but, oh, the thought of the judgment day! Her mother never broke the Sabbath; and, when the last trumpet sounds, her mother will arise and go with all the righteous; and if she lies still, she will be separated from her mother for ever. Oh, the anguish of her heart! If she arises when she hears the last trumpet, she will be sent, she thinks, to the blackness of darkness for ever and ever. She sees no way of escape. Where will she hide from the eye of Him who can see in the darkness as well as in the light? She weeps bitterly, till at last sleep, as in former days, comes to her relief.

In the morning, when her sister awakes her, Jenny starts up somewhat confused, and cries: "O my mother, my mother, is she dead?"

Her sister tells her that the doctor has done her mother good; she was greatly better, and wished to see Jenny. But sorrow and joy had followed too closely on one another for little Jenny, and she fainted away. In a little time, however, she was all right, and she runs to her mother's bedside and sobs out—"Mother, are ye no deid?"

"No, dear Jenny, dry your tears; God is very pitiful and full of mercy. He has not only spared your mother, but has also sent you the gift of a little brother." So saying, she removed the bed-clothes, and showed a lovely baby boy. Janet is transported; she fondly kisses both his cheek and chin, till her mother says—"Jenny, ye maun be canny, or ye'll hurt him. You maun be tender and kind to him, and you maun thank God for his great kindness to you and me, and love Him with all your heart. You know it is good to render thanks to God."

"Mother, if I begin to love God and keep the Sabbath day, will God love me yet?"

"My dear bairn, God does not wait till you love Him. He loved you when you were born, and though you have done many things to grieve Him, He still loves you, and has given you all that you have, and He has restored your mother when He might have closed her eyes in death; and he has also given you the gift of a little brother, and a father to work for you till you can work for yourself. All this He has done to show you how much He loves you, and that you may love Him who first loved you."

Poor little Jenny, there is a ray of hope rising in her heart; shall she see God on that awful judgment day and not be afraid? The day-star has not yet arisen in her heart, far less the noonday sun; but any one who has travelled along an unknown road in a dark night and has seen the first streak of day, and felt the calm soothing hope that the day-star, the forerunner of the noonday sun, is not far off, will be able from his own experience to understand Jenny's present feelings.

VI.

The Daily Round.

HITHERTO we have followed little Jenny in the bosom of her family, but now we come to a place where two roads cross each other; and Jenny goes one way, and her parents, and brothers, and sisters go another. We leave them for the present, and will only meet with them occasionally in their life's journey, but we purpose to follow little Jenny a little further. Now she has set her face Zionward, and is on her way thither. And if God, who is dealing with the spirits of all flesh, can use the record of His long-suffering mercy and goodness to her for a help to any one who is striving against sin, the end for which it is written will be accomplished, and the glory be given to His name for ever and ever.

Jenny's father came of a line of pious ancestors, and in matters of religion and home discipline, he was very strict. Her mother was like-minded in religious matters, and they ordered their household in much the same fashion as their ancestors had done. On the Saturday night preparations for the Day of Rest were made as far as possible. The vegetables for the morrow's dinner were prepared, the potatoes washed, and other household duties attended to, so that these might not interfere with the sacredness of the day. The Sabbath must be remembered; no work must be done; the house is made tidy, clean clothes are laid out, and on the "blest morning" all are early astir. While the porridge is boiling the family engage in worship; at half-past nine the father and all the children who are able set out for the church, each having a bit of pease-bannock in his or her pocket. It is a long way down to Yarrow Kirk, and it will be five o'clock in the afternoon before they get home again, hungry enough for the meal which they will find ready for them.

Dinner over, the dishes are set aside, to be washed on the Monday. Father then says—"Now, bairns, take your seats and tell your mother the text." All do their best, and father follows up, explaining and supplying what has been omitted; the mother lends an attentive ear, sharing in the fatness and marrow on which the husband and father had been feeding. Those of the bairns who can read are then set to learn a few verses of the Proverbs and a verse of a psalm, while the younger ones repeat to their father what mother had taught them during the day. Again, later on, they assemble round the fire, and the father takes down the Shorter Catechism, and, beginning with the mother, all the questions are put and answered, even to the Apostles' Creed and graces at the end, finishing with the Lord's Prayer. After supper, the old big Bible is laid down, mother locks the door, and the head of the household lifts the Book and reverently looks around. " Bairns," he says, " compose yourselves, and let us worship God ; and pay attention to what is read, and mind your notes." Each one was expected to mind a portion of what was read.

After reading, a psalm is sung, the father giving out the line ; and together they kneel in prayer and thanksgiving. The bairns are sent to the closet for private prayer, and then to bed, where they are not allowed to converse, but are told to repeat hymns and psalms, beginning in order with the one whose head lay in the direction of the rising sun. " The voice of rejoicing and salvation is in the tabernacles of the righteous."

On Monday morning, John is up by four o'clock. Before going out, he bends the knee and renders thanks for the mercies of the past night, he asks strength for the day, then proceeds with a cheerful heart to his labours, knowing that it is the will of God that in the sweat of his face he should eat his bread. Some time after, mother rises; water for the porridge is put on; baby is dressed, suckled, and laid in the cradle. By this time the older children are dressed. Tibbie takes down the Bible, reads a few verses, and engages shortly in prayer. One of the bairns is sent to the field with the father's porridge, and then all hands set to work.

In the evening John finds one or two of the children waiting his arrival at the burn, bringing a towel with them that he may use it as he washes his face ; and coming home, he finds everything neat and clean. Supper is on the table, and the bairns vie with each other in attending to their father's wants. As he is seated in the big chair in the corner, one climbs up on its back and combs his hair, another unbuttons his " cuitikens " or spats, and relieves the wearied feet of the clay-covered shoes. Then all are arranged round the supper table. " Now, bairns," he says, " close your eyes and lift up your hands, and let us ask God's blessing on the food His own hands have spread on the table." It is not easy for hungry boys to keep soldier-like position during the long grace, but they succeed wonderfully well. Then no one leaves the table till thanks is returned. Afterwards John lies back in his big chair, and takes a nap, while Tibbie and the girls clear away the dishes; after which, if it is summer, the bairns may all run out for play; if winter, they are employed in some useful way—the elder girls learn to spin, the boys to knit mittens.

At John's right hand is a shelf on which you may find the following books: 'Boston's Works,' 'The Confession of Faith,' 'The Solemn League and Covenant,' 'Life of Colonel Gardiner,' Bunyan's 'Pilgrim's Progress,' 'The Marrow of Modern Divinity,' Baxter's 'Saint's Rest,' Doddridge's 'Rise and Progress,' 'Robinson Crusoe,' 'Jack o' the Beanstalk,' a few ballads, the big Bible, and the 'Shorter Catechism.'

All the house is now in order. Tibbie takes her stocking and sits down beside her husband and awaits his waking, to hear and give the news of the day. He will by and bye take from the shelf one or other of the books named and read aloud till eight o'clock. Then all is put aside, the Bible laid down on the table, the door locked, worship engaged in as already described, and all retire to rest.

Thus these humble Christians try to train up their children in the fear of the Lord, in the faith and hope that when they are old they may not depart from it. The training of Jenny in this atmosphere will account for much in her history which is yet to follow.

Take my life, dear Lord, and raise it,
Wholly Thine so let it be;
Filled each moment from Thy fulness,
Moulded, guided, ruled by Thee.

All the mingled broken story
Of the past Thou readest well,
All the changeful shade and sunshine
Of the future thou canst tell.

Glad and free with Thee I leave them,
All my longings lost in One.
Higher, closer, closer draw me
To Thyself till years are done.

The new cottage had been at length completed, the smearing-house was left, and the family had occupied their more comfortable dwelling for some months. The elder children had gone to service—Nannie to Tinnis, Bell to Dr Clarkson's at Selkirk, and John to Fastheugh. Willie was engaged on the farm, and he, Janet, Nellie, and baby Robert were those left at home.

It was a day in the month of March, and snow still

covered the ground. Dinner was over, and Tibbie
had just got the dishes washed and a good peat fire
put on, so that it might be burned clear when her
husband came home at night cold and weary. Jenny
is rocking the cradle, and singing a lullaby to her
little brother. As pussy had taken the place of her
flower garden, now her baby brother had taken
pussy's place; she finds by his sweet smile that he
can in a measure return her love, and she is not only
satisfied but delighted as she sings—

> Hush, my dear, lie still and slumber,
>   Holy angels guard thy bed;
> Richest blessings without number
>   Gently fall upon thy head.

Her joy is great, she not only loves the little
one, but she is beginning to think well of the
Giver, and would like if she could love God as well
as she loves her mother. In the meantime her cup
is full; she knits her garter, rocks the cradle, and
sings. That afternoon her mother requires to bake,
and, on putting the bakeboard on the table at the
window, she looks out and sees a stranger making
for the door. He is a tall man; his hat is drawn
well over his brow. A shepherd's plaid is wrapped
round him so close that little is seen of his features
but his nose, and two dogs follow close on his heels.
He is a shepherd, there is no doubt; but what brings
him here? He does not rap at the door, but, in a
homely way, pushes it open, makes his way along
the passage, and with a muffled voice—for he speaks
through the plaid—asks:

" Hoo are a' the gude folk here the day, if I am no ower bold to speir ? "

"Thank you, we are all well," replied mother; "but I'm at a loss to know who it is that asks; but come in, honest man, and take a seat; we are commanded not to be forgetful to entertain strangers, for some have entertained angels unawares!"

" Weel, I wat I am a stranger, so I'll juist have to tell ye whae I am, and then I'll let ye ken my eerand. My name is Rob Shortreed. I'm a herd, I leeve across the Yarrow, on the ither side o' the hill, and the name o' oor hoose is the Hertloup, a bit ayont Altrive, where Wattie Amos leeves. Ye see my auld mother keeps my hoose, and we've been in the way o' keepin' a lassie in the simmer months, to herd the cow and be company for my mother; for ye'll understaund I'm often away frae hame—at clippin's and spainin' the lambs and attending fairs; and as tinklers and sic like gentry are aye comin' aboot the place, it takes mair than yin to watch them, baith in the hoose and oot the hoose; for they're a gey tarry-fingered set. I heard the ither day that ye had some auld farrant lasses, and I'm come to hire yin o' them if we can agree about the wages. I never gi'e ony less than a dizen o' shillin's for the half year, and I never gi'e ony mair."

"As for my bairns, honest man," said Tibbie, "they have faults like other folk's. Ye may gi'e them a good advice, and also use the rod o' correction, but we cannot put a new heart in them—that's God's work. But be that as it may, I'm sorry to say that ye have been ower late o' comin', for my two oldest lasses are both at service; and we got word just last night that they were staying on in their places; and though I am very sorry for your auld mother, ye see I cannot help her."

"Aweel," said Rob, "I dinna ken hoo to gang hame and tell her, for she was wonderfu' lifted up wi' the hope o' getting yin o' your lasses, for we had an awfu' botheration wi' the yin we had last simmer. Ye see, I gaed doon to Selkirk fair, and hired what ye wad ca' a faisable-eneuch lookin' lassie, and for a while she did no that ill; but, comin' frae Selkirk, she thocht our hoose was awfu' dull, and the day afore the Common Ridin' there, when my mother was milking the cow, she slippit oot her bits o' duds and ran strecht off hame; and a' the airt we had we couldna' coax her back. My mother had a terrible time o't, I can tell 'e—what wi' the wunnin' o' the peats, and lookin' after the cow's hay, and the paidlin' o' the tatties and cabbage, and watchin' the tinklers and packmen and beggars, it was eneuch to put her daft. I railly dinna ken hoo ta gang hame, for she'll no sleep a wink the nicht."

Little Jenny listens to all that is said, and her tender heart is moved with pity for the old woman, and on the impulse of the moment she says—

"I'll gang and help the man's mother."

"You! bairn," replied Tibbie; "what could you do? I'm sure you're fit for naething."

"O," says Rob, "I think she would do rale weel; I'm fer mista'en if she's no the yin that Wattie

Laidlaw speaks sae muckle aboot. Is her name Jenny ? "

" Weel, man, that is her name; but she's just a bairn, no eight years old till the fourth of June; and more than that, she has got no schooling to speak of; we are so far from any school here, and I am just giving her a bit lesson at odd times mysel'. Her gang to service! it would be nonsense to think about it. Na, na, that'll no dae."

" Hoot, woman," said Rob, " that's a ditch that can easy be jumped. Div ye see my brother Tam is a wricht, and has a bit shop at the end o' the hoose, and though he's often workin' at the ferm-toons in the simmer, he's generally hame at nicht; and now, in the spring-time, he's thrang makin' new kists for the servants, the lads and lasses that are flittin'. Of coorse, they like to gang decent hame to a new place; and, ye see, Wattie Laidlaw often comes ower to gi'e Tam a bit hand. They're baith guidish scholars, and it wad be naethin' to them to gi'e the lassie a lesson. In fack, I think Wattie would raither like it. The simmer months sune pass away, and then ye can school her through the winter. Here, my little wumman," said Rob, " here's a shillin' for your erles. Ye'll no can wade Yarrow, but Wattie Laidlaw is comin' on Tuesday, and he can stilt Yarrow when it's geyin big, and he'll cairry ye ower on his back; and you'll get hame at mid-term to see your mother. Guid nicht, Tibbie; I'm gled that I've got this business settled."

" It's no settled, Rob. You must not think that; for I'm sure that her faither 'll no let her; and though you have kind o' forced the erles into her hand, she's but a bairn, and it will not stand law."

"Keep up yer heart, Tibbie; my mother will be gude till her;" and with that Rob whistles on his dogs, and away he goes.

Poor Tibbie, as she shuts the door, feels as if her head were turned. She will tell Janet that she ought to have refused the arles, but she meets her mother with a face beaming with delight.

"Mother, come and see how rich baby is; I put the shilling in his little fat hand; and see how he hauds it; and do ye ken when I come hame at Martinmas wi' my wage I'll buy you a new goon and my faither a new Sabbath-day hat, and Robert will then be walking, and I will buy him his first shoon."

Willie, turning to her, says, "An' will ye gi'e my faither siller when he gangs doon to Selkirk, to buy me a penny trump,[1] for I can whustle 'Cawdor Fair?'"

The poor mother's breast is heaving with perturbation, but she feels that she cannot mar the joy of the young heart which she would ever wish to soothe— she will wait till she hears what John says. She retires to the closet to meet with Him who is ever ready to help all that come unto Him in time of need.

Evening comes, and Willie runs off to meet his father with the news. "Faither," he says, "div ye ken oor Jen's gaun to service?" Janet also meets her father, and tells him about the shilling and her big wage—a whole dozen of shillings—and

_____
[1] A Jew's harp.

what she purposes to buy when she comes home at the term.

"You have a loving heart, my little woman," said John, "but where is your mother?"

Tibbie had some difficulty in putting on a bright face, and John was quick enough to see that her eyes were a little watery. "Well, gudewife, what's happened, he asked? One would think from your face that ye have had a scuffle with the Philistines; if so, I hope you have come off victorious."

"Weel, gudeman, ye're no far wrang; the battle has been a gey hard ane; but the giant is not killed; I have been waiting for you to give me a hand."

John lends an attentive ear while Tibbie relates all that passed with Rob Shortreed, and she adds, "It makes my heart sair when I look at my bairn, and see her joy; she just looks like a bit innocent lamb gambolling with its companions on the green hill-side, all unconscious of the butcher's knife."

"So ye think that Rob intends to butcher Jenny?"

"Now, gudeman, that's like you to laugh at me; but ye ken as well as me that there are more ways o' killing than cutting the throat."

"True, Tibbie; but ye forget the proverb that ye often use—'That the de'il gets only the length o' his tether,' and another ye often repeat is—'That He is abune that guides the gullie.' If ye can look at Rob Shortreed just as a tool in the hand of Him who appoints the bounds of the habitations of all people, you would be quite willing to let the lassie follow the leading of Providence."

" Ah, man, but ye ken little about the yearning of a mother's heart."

" Well, maybe that's true, Tibbie, but ye must confess that I ken something of a father's feeling ; for I have often thought if I had been a rich man my bairns would have been fools. When you and me came thegither we had the hope on baith sides o' a pickle siller coming our way, but ye see it took wings and flew away. God, I daur say, saw it was too dangerous a commodity to trust you and me with, and when He gave us offspring He took the burden of their being on Himself, and it's no for you and me to thwart His purposes, but just to work along with Him. When I look on our bairns and think that the Lord is their father, a better father than I am or ever can be, I feel the burden lifted in a measure off my back, and it would ease your motherly feeling to believe that His heart is more tender than yours. Just let Jenny follow in the path God is leading, and you'll see it will be all well with both her and us in the end. And if she should be ill used, she has yet a father's house to come back to, and a mother's heart to welcome her ; and in the meantime dinna you look sad, so as wound the bit tender heart before the time, but look as bright as you can, and encourage her."

" Weel, gudeman, as you think it right that Janet should go from under our roof while she is yet a bairn, I bow as I ought to your decision ; but it is a gey rent to my heart. It's no easy for a mother to act the hypocrite. May the Lord have mercy on us ! "

VII.

Off to Hard Service.

THE following Monday, Tibbie makes up a bundle of clothing, and tells Jenny that she has put in her doll, saying it will keep her from wearying when she is herding the cow, but she must not play with it on the Sabbath-day. Jenny blushed and looked down, but said nothing, and her mother added, "And I have put in your carritch (Catechism) too. Though ye canna read big words you can say questions off by heart, but look on when ye're saying them; it'll help ye tae read. And pay great attention when Tam and Wattie gi'e ye a lesson, an' dinna forget tae say your prayers nicht and mornin', an' your psalms and hymns till ye fa' asleep. And aye be biddable, Jenny; and when ye're in a fault dinna try tae excuse yoursel', but try tae dae better; and aye dae it the very way your mistress bids ye. Never take your ain way, 'master-will is good work.' Your faither will gi'e ye some guid coonsel after he gets his supper."

Bed time comes on, and poor Janet feels a pain

at her heart. How can she part with her baby brother, and miss the sight of his golden hair and blue eyes and rosy cheeks, his little fat arms that have often been stretched out to her when holding up his dear mouth to be kissed? And then Willie and little Nellie, and father and mother—oh, she never loved them half so much as she does this night.

"How foolish I was tae say I wad gang," she murmurs, "hoo wrang it was tae take the erles; but I dinna like tae say now that I winna gang. Oh, what will I dae? After I put off my claes, before I gang tae bed, I'll slip oot and rin amang the snaw, and I'll take a sair throat, and I'll no be able tae rise."

Poor Janet, she indeed does as she purposes: she runs naked amongst the snow, she rubs it on her breast and face and arms; she is sure to be ill, and not able to go. Then she slips into her bed; and no one knows the state of her mind, or what she has done.

Contrary to her expectation and her wish, she wakes in the morning refreshed, having slept soundly after her snow bath. But her heart is sore; the porridge will not go down, her mother observes; and she easily understands the reason; her heart is sore likewise, but she tries to be cheerful. She speaks of having something fine for dinner when her lassie comes home with her twelve shillings, but Janet cannot smile. She thinks her mother does not love her, or she would not be so cheery, and this adds to her grief.

Now it is time for Janet to go. Her mother, to save a sad parting with her little daughter, sends Willie with her to carry her bundle. Jenny takes farewell of her baby brother, sisters, and mother; her father had kissed her and blessed her in the morning before going out to his work. She looks round the house, pussy fawns on her, she strokes its back and rubs its ears, and then, with short steps, she makes for the door; then a woeful feeling comes over her, but she cannot cry. Oh! if her mother would but look sorrowful, Janet could endure the rest; but her mother acts the merciful hypocrite, and smiles as she bids her lassie good-bye.

It is not possible for me to describe Jenny's anguish. Oh, let mothers be true to nature; love never hurts any one; open rebuke is better than secret love. Like "Lucy o' the Glen," Janet went slowly down the burnside with her flitting; thinking that "Fareweel, Jenny, was ilka bird's sang."

Wattie Laidlaw was at the water-side according to appointment, and he gets Janet on his back, and her bundle in his teeth, and stilts the Yarrow. Her mother, from the door, watches till they are safely landed on the other side of the stream, and then she shuts herself up in the closet. Wattie and Jenny climb the hill, then descend on the other side, pass Altrive, and proceed along the face of the hill. At last they arrive at Hartleap, the abode of Rob Shortreed and his mother Katie Nicol.

In those days it was considered out of place for any one but the Laird's wife to be called "mistress;"

even among the farmers it was always "gudeman" and "gudewife." Katie Nicol was a very little woman. On this day she wore a yellow petticoat, a blue and yellow gown, and a white and blue apron, all made from wool of her own spinning; the yellow her own dyeing, from stoneraw gathered from the rocks on the hill-side. On her head was a white "mutch," or cap, with black ribbons tied round it.

"Katie," says Wattie, "I've brocht hame your servant, and she'll no make a fool of you through being ower big."

"Weel, Wattie, I never was big mysel', but I could aye get through my wark as weel as some o' thae saft butter lumps; but I'm a wee doubtfu' if that bit craitur'll be worth her meat; she's no the size o' a pair o' mittens."

"Weel, Katie, that is at least a sinless infirmity," replied Wattie; "and one that will daily mend, if ye feed her weel."

"Weel, that's the first thing a new servant is set to, to see how she eats;" and so saying, Katie cuts a slice of pease-bannock, and spreads some butter on it with her thumb, and says—"Here, lassie, if ye never get onything waur than that ye'll have nae cause to compleen."

Poor little Jenny! Her heart is sore; she sees none of the kindly ways of her mother in her new mistress, and though she was not accustomed to get butter on her bread, she thought Katie's thumb did not look too clean when she spread it; so it was "raither ill to gang doon."

Katie observed that Jenny was making but slow

progress with the bread. " I'm thinkin'," says she, " if ye work nae better than that ye'll no need to be ca'd oot o' a kailyaird for a' the cabbage ye'll eat; but maybe ye're like ower mony o' your kind, ower fine brocht up. See, there's a soup milk to sinde it doon wi'."

We will leave Jenny with her pease-bannock, and give the reader a description of the herd's house at " the Hartleap." In that time you entered by a door in the centre of the house; on the left hand of the passage was the cow; a little further on there was the hay neuk, and at the far end of the passage a door leading into the family apartment. Here there was a window of four small panes, a fire on the floor near the centre of the place, and a hole in the roof by which the peat-reek, after coursing through the place, found its way outside. On one side of the fire is a long chair that will seat three or four persons; on the opposite side is the peat-neuk, which is refilled from the stack every morning. The furniture consists of two box beds, a big press and dresser, a few three-footed stools, and a table. Between the beds is a door that leads to the other part of the dwelling, what is called the " ben-a-hoose." As you enter, that on your right hand is the potato bin, boarded up with a few rough deals. This will hold a quantity of potatoes, which are covered with hay to protect them from frost, and the bin is supplied now and again during the winter from the pit in the garden. In a row at the wall, stand the oatmeal barrel, the pot barley barrel, the flesh barrel, a firkin with salt butter; and then there are the kirn (churn), the bakeboard, the girdle, the kail pot, porridge pot, the water stoups, the washing tub, the dish boyne, and a rough deal resting on two big stones, on which are milk plates (large vessels of common earthenware), with milk in them.

On the opposite side, at the back of the beds, is a large chest in which are contained various articles, such as blankets and Sabbath-day clothes; there is a wheel for spinning woollen yarn, a little wheel for spinning lint, the reel, a set of cards for carding the wool, a set of clots, a bundle of wool, and a wecht [1] full of rowans, ready for spinning.

Katie takes Jenny through the house and shows her where everything is kept, and says to her— " Now, see that ye aye put things where ye find them; see, tak' the dish ben and gether up a wheen tatties, and tak' them to the burn and wash them, and bring them in and scrape them for the supper. Ye maun learn that there's nae sittin' and coontin' fingers here."

The snow was still lying on the ground, and Jenny's feet were wet and cold; and ere she got the potatoes washed her little fingers were like carrots. However, she managed to scrape the potatoes, and they are washed, put into the pot, and hung on the swey over the fire. That being done, Katie says— " Now, gether up the peelins' for the cow's supper; see, there's a lantern, licht the bit cannle that's in it, and get the milk-handy, and come ben and haud the cannle till I milk the cow."

By this time the potatoes are ready for being

---

[1] An article shaped like a riddle, the bottom covered with skin.

beaten, and a good supper of potatoes and milk is enjoyed. Then the dishes are washed and put past. Rob has been playing the fiddle, with which he occupies his spare time; Wattie and Tam were talking over Dr Russell's sermon, under whose ministry Tam sat. Katie reminds them that it is time for worship, which Tam very reverently conducts; but Jenny wonders that he does not ask for their "notes."

Katie then says, " Now, lassie, gang away to yer bed, and I will be in beside you if I had the fire raked, and the porridge pot hung on to be ready in the morning."

Jenny looks bewildered, and is in great trouble. She had promised her mother to mind and say her prayers; but there is no closet here, and Katie is ben the house getting the porridge pot and meal box, and setting bye her wheel. Where or what will little Jenny do for a dark place to say her prayers, where no eye but God's can see, and no ear but His can hear? She might find a place at the back o' the door, but the men have gone out to look round them before going to bed, and they may come in while she is there. What will she do? She cannot go to bed without saying her prayers; and at last she ventures to the back of the door and repeats the Lord's Prayer as fast as she can. As yet she did not know what it was to pray, but she did that which she knew to be right at the time, and her conscience was at rest. Then she went to bed and slept soundly. Oh, how many never get beyond " saying their prayers," but Jenny learned to pray and to love Him to whom she prayed, and waited patiently for His answer.   She could say in truth :

> When all thy mercies, O my God !
>   My rising soul surveys,
> Transported with the view, I'm lost
>   In wonder, love, and praise.
>
> To all my weak complaints and cries
>   Thy mercy lent an ear,
> Ere yet my feeble thoughts had learned
>   To form themselves in prayer.

STILTING THE YARROW.

VIII.

Boston and the Ghost.

THE inmates of Hartleap are all up by five in the morning, and Katie sets Jenny to work.

"Here, lassie," she says, "look ahint the door, and ye'll get a heather buzzim; soop the fluir, and mind an' gang into every neuk; nane o' yer half-dune wark, and take out the ashes — see, there's a wecht, and then cairry in peats and fill the peat neuk. I'll gang and make the beds, milk the cow, and make the porridge; an' after ye cairry in the peats, gang to the back o' the hoose, and ye'll see a hurl-barrow; bring it to the door, and ye'll get a graip and a paidle at the hay neuk, and gang and clean up the byre, an' see that ye dinna slaister the entry, haddin' folk cairryin' in shairn on their feet."

Poor little Janet was nearly knocked up before she got her porridge. To push the wheelbarrow was a sore job, for her short arms with difficulty reached the shafts of the barrow; but with many a zigzag and couping over she reached the dunghill. Breakfast is over, but no worship, no closet. Still Janet must say her prayers, but where can she find a corner out of sight? She runs up the burn, and to her great delight she finds a little hollow, and here she kneels down and says, " Lord, be merciful to me a sinner," and runs back before she is missed.

On her return, Katie says, " See lassie, be clever, and get the dishes washed, and gang oot into the yaird and cut some greens, and take the graip and howk up some leeks and take them to the burn and wash them, and bring them in and shear them for the kail, and then take the tatty creel and wale a wheen tatties and wash them at the burn—and dinna gang as if ye were chasing a snail, and blawin' away at your hands—an' be active at your wark, and that'll warm them—and I'll hing on the kail pot and bring ben my wheel, for I maun gang on wi' my spinnin' to get the yairn away to the weaver afore we begin to cast the peats. Ye see the tatties are to be cut—div ye ken hoo to cut tatties for settin' without destroying them? Weel, what was I sayin'? Oh aye, the tatties maun be ready for Rob to plant after lambing time, for he will be needin' you to gang to the hill wi' him to cairry warm milk for some o' the silly yins, and bring hame on yer back the dead yins—no for their flesh, for that's no worth the eatin', but for their skins. Did ye ever skin a lamb? But I needna ask quais- tins; you'll have that to learn like ither things. O lassie, you're just like a bird half oot o' the shell— and then the cow will have to be oot to the grass— and you'll have to herd, and watch that she does na gang ower the mairch when you're paidlin' the tatties and cabbage—and b' that time the hay will be in hand, and the theekin' for the hoose and the peak stack, and the hay stack, and the hay ropes to make, in case the rain rots or the wund blaws it a' away. Then or ever we ken what we're daein', the tatties will be to lift and pit, and the cabbage to pit, and the peats to get in—so your doll 'll get a gude sleep, and you'll get time to play wi' it when ye gang hame. It wad be wicer like if yer mother was trainin' ye to make something to cover yer naked back, for I hear that ye're gey bare-like at hame—a plooghman's faimily have never onything to spare, but are aye juist leevin' atween the hand an' the mooth.

Jenny's face flushed, for she felt it was partly true, but she said, " My mother says we dinna need braw claes or siller to take us to Heaven."

" That's true, my wummin, but whae div 'e think 'll get there ? "

" The Elect," says Janet.

" Yes ; but whae's the Elect ? "

" It's just them that gets there ; and when I learn to read, my mother says that I maun read Boston's ' Fourfold State.' It tells a' aboot election."

" Oh aye, lass, Bowston was a holy man ; they say he had an awfu' battle wi' the de'il when he laid the ghaist of Whuphoose Janet."

" My mother says there's nae ghaists, and that we'll never see onything waur than oursel's."

" My lassie, ye'll have to learn that there's as wice folk in the world as yer mother ; and I have heard it frae some that wadna tell a lee, that the story of Bowston layin' the ghaist was as true as there's a mune in the lift.

"I never heard the story ye're speakin' aboot," says Janet.

"The story, lassie! Did ye never hear that the miller at Whuphoose[1] was blamed for killin' a packman, and hidin' his deid body under the mill-wheel, for the sake o' his pack and his purse? So ye see that the packman's ghaist, like a' murdered folk, couldna rest, but was aye seen atween the miller's hoose and the kirk, and the folk was that feared that they durstna gang to the kirk. So Bowston asked the folk to pray for him, and he would gang the next nicht and speak to the ghaist. So on the neist Sabbath day he tell'd the folk they would never see the ghaist more, for he said it was the de'il, and he had laid him. But Bowston wad never tell what he said to the ghaist and the de'il, but it was thocht that he had had a gey tussle wi' them, an' the ghaist was never mair seen. But you're forgettin' what I was sayin' tae 'e—after you get the denner things washed up, ye'll need to caird me some rowens, for I maun get on wi' my spinnin'. Has your mother ever lairn'd 'e to caird?"

"Yes," said Janet meekly, "but I'm no gude at it."

"Weel, I can believe 'e; what are ye gude at, I wad like to ken? See and watch the sand-glass till I bring ben the wheel, and turn it whenever it rins oot, and put a stroke on the back o' the door; see, here's a bit cauk (chalk); for if 'e dinna turn it whan it rins oot we winna ken whan to pit on the tatties for the denner."

Janet was at a loss to understand what was said

---

[1] Hopehouse, in Ettrick.

about the sand-glass; she looked at something on the table, and then looked at the door; but what it all meant, or what she had to do with it, she could not guess.

Katie says, "Lassie, did ye never see a sand-glass? Where have 'e been a' yer days? I needna ask that—in some ootlandish place, nae doot; wummin, ye're as ignarint as a peat. How does yer mother ken what o'clock to have the denner ready?"

"My mother has a wag-at-the-wa'."

"Pity me! I may gi'e up the spinnin' and dae naething but tell 'e the names o' things, and what they are for. See here; turn aboot and look—an' mind what I tell 'e, and no haud me aye speakin' tae 'e. See, that's a sand-glass; div 'e see 't?—it rins doon frae where it is the noo every five meen-its, and ye juist turn it up whan it runs oot; and see, there's the bit cauk; every time ye turn it, pit a stroke on the back o' the door, and whan ye have twal' strokes pit a cross stroke, and that makes the hoor—and, mind ye, ask Rob when he gangs oot what o'clock it is in his watch, and then begin to turn the sand-glass. Div 'e understand?"

This is only a very imperfect detail of Janet's daily labour, and what work she is to look forward to, and of which she gets her full share. Her fingers get chilblains, the glands in the pit of her arms swell, she feels pains in her shoulders, in her back, and knees; and when she is bidden to run here and there her little limbs will not obey. Once, and only once, when she is scolded and called lazy, she ventures to say, "My legs are sore;" and all the sympathy she gets is that it's just growing pains, and she must learn to bear them. I may state here that when it was a sunny day the sand-glass was not needed, but Janet had another lesson to learn.

Katie, on another day, says, "Lassie, gang oot an' step yer shadow; come in an' tell me, an' we'll see if it is time to put on the tatties for the denner."

Poor Janet had often with her brothers and sisters played at trying to catch her shadow, but what it was to "step her shadow," or what it had to do with the potatoes for the dinner, she could not comprehend. So she stood still, looking at Katie, and then at the door.

Katie's patience was exhausted, and she broke out— "Lassie, 'e wad provoke a sant! Wull I have to leeve my wheel an' gang oot and let e' see hoo to step yer shadow? it'll be a lang time or I get my spinnin' dune at this rate. See, run to the door— I wonder if ye can see the sun abune yer stuipid heid. Now, mind what I tell 'e—when it's a sunny day we dinna need the sand-glass—juist you gang oot and stand in the sunshine, and mark the place where yer shadow reaches tae—div' e' understand that?—and then coont hoo mony steps it is to the place yer shadow reaches tae, and then come in an' tell me, an' I'll ken what o'clock it is—and when the sun is richt abune yer heid, ye'll have nae shadow— it will be twal' o'clock."

Janet tries to please Katie, but it is not easily done. Still she takes all quietly, and minds her mother's counsel, never to speak back.

Time moves on, but to Janet the days seem to go very slowly by; she counts the days and the weeks till she will get home with her big wage. Oh, how happy will she be then! In the meantime she has to be up at five in the morning, and she feels so sleepy she does not know what to do. But she is at service, and will always need to be a servant. Will she always need to rise at five, and not get to bed till ten? She sees no alternative, so she tries to comfort herself by thinking that she will get a long sleep in the grave before the last day comes.

Let no one say that my story is overdrawn; no, it is not so. Perhaps those for whom it is written will drop a tear of sympathy over the hard lot of little Janet in her early days. There is One who neither slumbers nor sleeps watching over the little slave, One who can bring good out of such bitter experience as she was passing through.

Summer is now come, and the cow gets out to the grass; and Janet has one whole day in seven to herd her. The Sabbath is strictly observed, at least by abstaining from outward work, and Janet gets a little rest; but it is a whole day sitting among the hills, from five o'clock in the morning till eight at night, trying to keep the Sabbath day holy by reading, or rather trying to read, the *Single Questions*, the only book she possessed. But there is no one to speak to, no one to give her a lesson; the little lambs on the hill-side are gambolling with their fellows, and sucking their mothers with great delight, but she is lonely and sad. Many strange thoughts would pass through her mind: she often wished that

God had made her a little lamb. She did not then know that she was a lamb of God's own flock, and the Good Shepherd was carrying all her sorrows in His own bosom, and would one day gather her with His arm, and Himself wipe all her tears away.

I think, when I read that sweet story of old,
   When Jesus was here among men,
How He called little children, as lambs to His fold,
   I should like to have been with them then.
I wish that His hands had been placed on my head,
   That His arm had been thrown around me,
And that I might have seen His kind look when He said,
   "Let the little ones come unto Me."

IX.

A Hurricane among the Hills.

HERE is much more connected with Janet's stay at Hartleap that we would like to record, but it would be too tedious to relate; so we pass on by taking notice of the following incident. It is midsummer. Rob has been away at the clipping of the sheep for ten days; Tam has been working at the farm for some weeks; Katie and Janet are all alone. The Hartleap stands among the hills, not in sight of any other dwelling, and sometimes weeks passed by without them seeing a human being, unless perhaps a tinker passing that way now and again. In the evenings Katie used to interest Janet with witch stories and wonderful tales about ghosts and fairies. One night the wind blew a hurricane, and Katie is in great terror. She thinks the de'il is let loose, and is sure that the house will be blown down, and she, and the cow, and the cat, and the old dog Trusty killed. Trusty had been her husband's companion, but the poor creature is now both deaf and blind, and it would be awful to see the poor creature smothered among the ruins. As the storm increases in fury, Katie trembles from head to foot; she leaves her spinning, and draws close to Janet, and says—

" Lassie, are ye no fear'd ? "

" No," says Janet, " I'm no fear'd; for my mother says that God walks on the wings of the wind and rides on the storm; my mother learned me that psalm that says, ' Fire and hail, snow and vapour, stormy wind, fulfilling His word.' They are all His servants, and they can only do what God bids them; and God is kind; and if we pray to Him, He will take care of us."

" But did yer mother never tell ye hoo God gave the de'il leave to raise the wund, and let it blaw doon the hoose on Job's bairns ? "

" Yes, my mother told me that the de'il said to God that Job was a selfish man, that he just pretended to love God for things God had given him, and that if God took them from him he would curse God; but God knew that Job loved Him, so God said to the de'il, I will allow you to take all these things from Job, but I will not allow you to kill him. So you see that the de'il canna hurt us, and if he should knock down the house, God can spare our lives, and give us another, just as he did to Job."

" Oh, lassie, ye are ower wice ; but div'e no hear hoo the hoose is creekin' ? Oh, I never heard sic a wund as that.

A great blast comes and carries away part of the roof. Katie clung to Janet and exclaimed, " Oh, preserve us, the hoose is doon ! "

"No," says Janet, "it's just the theekin' blawn off, and ye see we are no deid."

The old woman trembled, and Janet commenced to cry. "Aye," says Katie, "I thocht you wad get fear'd if the hoose fell."

"I am no fear'd," says Janet; "but I'm vexed to see you so frichtened, and I canna help greeting for you."

The storm abated, and no more damage was done by it. Janet's tears fell like dew from the fountain of love on the hardened heart of the old woman; and on the morrow, when Janet got her forenoon piece of pease-bannock, it was accompanied with a slice of cheese and kind words from the old woman. "See, Janet, my little wummin, there's yer piece; gang oot and sit doon at the hay-stack, and watch the cow while ye're eatin' it." Not less soothing were Katie's words to Janet than Janet's tears were to Katie. This was the first gentle tone that had sounded in the little servant's ears since she left her mother, and she felt that even the wheelbarrow became somewhat lighter. Here we may see how truly love begets love, and also that love makes labour light.

The effects of the tempest had to be looked to, and Tom and Wattie Laidlaw have been busy redding up the workshop and putting up a temporary shed, into which the furniture is removed, also the cow and the cat and old Trusty. The house is taken down, and the neighbouring shepherds volunteer to lend a hand in putting up a new one. There are Jamie Scott, of Eldinhope; Jamie and Wat Amos, of

Altrive; Sandy Laidlaw, of Bowerhope; and John Beattie, of the Berrybush; and occasionally some others.

Rob and Tam, Wattie Laidlaw, and Jamie Amos have cast the divots,[1] the foundation is laid, then a row of stones and two rows of divots, and so on till the walls are the proper height; then Wattie Laidlaw and Tam put on the roof, and Rob and Jamie thatch it with rushes and divots. Janet and Katie have been carrying ha'clay from the burn, and which is mixed with cow droppings to plaster the inside of the house with. A larger window is put in, a sort of fire-place is formed with large stones, the furniture is replaced, and a separate byre erected for the cow. How fine all things look! Tam brings home an eight-day clock. If Janet was puzzled with the sand-glass, Katie is more so with the clock, for this is the first one she has seen. It is Janet's part to teach her how it showed the time; and she found it was no easy task she had in hand.

Wattie Laidlaw has learned from Katie what had passed between her and Janet on that fearful night when the wind blew off the roof; and one night he said to Janet, " The de'il did a gude turn to blaw doon the hoose."

Janet looked Wattie in the face as if she was surprised to hear him say so, but she said nothing. Wattie was anxious to draw out of Janet what her real thoughts were about the wind and the de'il. He said, " Janet, is not this a fine house? It's a pity the de'il did not blaw it doon sooner."

[1] Square pieces of turf.

Janet was thinking, but she did not like to speak all that was in her mind at the time; but, being pressed, she at last said—" It was not the de'il that did the good, it was God. He saw that we needed a new hoose, so he first bade the wind blaw doon the auld one."

Janet was reckoned "a sort of curiosity" among the shepherds, and many a puzzling question was put to her. But the heart even of a child knows its own bitterness, and a stranger intermeddles not with its joy. From the first day she entered Hartleap, Janet carried a sorrow that none but God knew, and now she has a joy that she can tell to none. In the midst of all the confusion God remembered Janet's sorrow, and provided for her a praying place. The byre is now entered by a separate door from the dwelling-house, and she can run in and shut the door and say her prayers. Oh, the joy that filled her heart. Truly a sparrow falleth not to the ground without our Heavenly Father's notice. Janet did not forget her mother's counsel that time when her lost cat returned, and she rendered thanks to God for giving her the byre to say her prayers in.

It is not our place or portion that makes us good or ill,
But it's the way we labour God's purpose to fulfil;
The question we're to answer when from this life we gang,
Is how each one in their station sang their own true sang.

X.

A Timely Rescue.

AS the days of her service at Hartleap are getting to an end, Janet's heart is getting a little lighter; she can count the weeks on her fingers—only ten, and then will come the happy day when she will go home with her twelve shillings. Till then she has sore work before her, but with the bright prospect of getting back to her father's house again, the time goes merrily past. The 11th of November, the term-day, has at length come round, and Janet gathers her few articles together, and ties them up in a little bundle. Her brother John has just arrived at Hartleap to bring home his sister. Katie thinks and says that they needed not to have been in such a hurry for a day or two. Rob says, "Here, lassie; here's yer wages. I promised ye a dizzen o' shillings, but as ye have pleased my mother, and aye did her bidding, and been quiet, here's fourteen shillings for you." Katie says, "And here's a pickle yairn to knit a pair of stockings;" and then she puts large pieces of bread and cheese in her hand, and says, "Janet, ye'll come back and see us, will ye na? Fare-ye-weel, lassie!"

Janet's heart was somewhat full, and she wept when she parted with the old woman; but, oh! the joy of going home with fourteen shillings to her mother absorbed every other thought. Her brother and she got to the side of the Yarrow; John had been told to wait till their father came with a horse to bring them through, but not coming so soon as they expected, and impatient to be home, they thought they would try and wade the stream, which that day had been rising higher than its ordinary level. A shepherd, observing their movements, and their danger, hastened to their rescue, threw his plaid from him, rushed into the water, and just in time laid hold of them as the stream was carrying them off their feet. What a narrow escape from drowning! This event made the home meeting more solemn, and more grateful thanks ascended to the Preserver of their lives.

Janet laid her fourteen shillings in her mother's lap, and then divided her bread and cheese among her brothers and sisters. Her mother said, " My dear little lassie, you deserve a new frock out of your hardly won wages, but your brother John is going away to a situation in Edinburgh, and I will need to take your wages to get him decently fitted out, but I will buy you a new frock when the cow calves, and I sell the butter."

Jenny loved her brother John, and said, " Mother, never mind me; make John right."

She was not without need of a new frock—the drugget one which she had worn all the summer sorely needed both washing and mending; but all her life Janet was more concerned about the needs of others than her own; so she was glad to have it in her power to help her brother.

Oh, that word "home!" Who can describe it? Janet is at home, seated at her father's fireside, himself in the old arm chair, her mother on the opposite side, Janet with her baby brother on her knee. Little Nellie, who sits next her mother, is in high glee, for Janet has given her the doll, all fresh after its long sleep at Hartleap. Willie and John strive a little with each other who is to be nearest their sister, and Janet's cup of joy is full. Will it ever taste so sweet again till they all meet in the heavenly home, where there will be no separation—when the dark waters of death have been crossed; when sustained by the Good Shepherd, and carried in His bosom to the Father's house of many mansions, as trophies of the travail of His own soul? All tears shall there be wiped away, and their sun shall no more go down, for the days of their mourning shall be ended. Gracious God, grant that it may be so!

It is eight o'clock; mother locks the door, father takes down the big Bible, and, with a look of inexpressible tenderness, says—"Now, bairns, compose yourselves, and let us worship God; and mind your notes." After singing four verses or so of a psalm, and reading a portion of the Word of God, they all kneel; and the good man out of the fulness of his heart pours out his thanksgiving to the Father in heaven for all His mercies towards them as a family, especially for His mercy in saving his thoughtless children that day from a watery grave. His feelings overcome him, and the whole family weep aloud. When they rise from their knees, Janet throws her arms round her father's neck, lays her head on his bosom and weeps, saying, "Faither, it was all my fault, I wanted John to wade the water, for I was wearying so to see my mother."

John kissed his little daughter; then they all sang part of the first hymn at the end of the Paraphrases, "Through hidden dangers, toils, and death." Then the children are sent to their prayers. How happy Janet was to find herself once more in their own closet!

Day after day passed by; Janet was a great help to her mother, her elder sisters being at service, but the motherly heart was moved to see her hacked hands and swelled fingers, and more so when she learned that the glands in her arm-pits were swollen and hard. She had suffered constant pain arising from that cause patiently; for Katie Nicol said they were just growing pains, and she must bear them till she is a woman.

We will here leave mothers to guess the anguish of Tibbie's heart. She is also grieved to learn that Janet had never got a lesson since the day she left home; so her mother resumes the teaching of her little daughter, and Janet is a very attentive scholar. Oh, how she longed to read for herself the stories of the Bible, but as yet she only knows the little words. When the other children are out playing, she takes down the big Bible, and manages to slip un-observed into the closet, and there she would sit

F

sometimes for hours, turning over the leaves, from the beginning to the end, reading the little words, and longing, or may I say praying? that she could read the holy book.

And thus day after day for three months did she pursue her task. At last one day while turning over the leaves of Matthew's Gospel, her eye was arrested by the story of Christ riding into Jerusalem on an ass. She commenced reading the chapter, and, to her astonishment, she found it quite easy to read to the end without spelling one word! She wondered why she could not read it long before this; it was so easy, and she turned to other portions and found them equally so. Her feeling at the time was that of shame that she had been so long in finding out that it was so easy, but she told no one; and her mother got great credit for the way in which Janet was now able to read.

In after years, when Janet had learned that there was nothing too hard for God, she gave Him all the glory for helping her so. Oh, how happy she is now. She commits to memory psalms and hymns; while her mother is spinning she sits by her side and repeats them, and thus they take sweet counsel together, and their hearts are made glad. But Janet has a deeper lesson to learn than to read: she must yield up her own will to the will of God, and follow the leading of His providence without murmuring.

XI.

As David and Jonathan.

EARLY in the spring of the year, on a cloudy, cold¦ afternoon, Tibbie is about to set down her wheel, Janet has washed her face, combed her hair, and put on a clean pinafore, as her wont was, and is about to sit down by her mother to read the lesson, when Willie comes running in, saying, "Mother! there's a man on a horse comin' up the burn-side."

A stranger coming to Dryhope in those days was a rare thing. This one is a man in working clothes, seated on an old white horse. He makes for the door and alights, ties his horse to the handle of the door, raps, and calls out, "Gudewife, may a stranger come in?"

Tibbie says, "If ye come peaceably, and in the name of the Lord, ye are welcome."

"Peaceably, good woman, for when God has made peace war is needless. The Lord has laid a burden on me and mine, and I am come to you to help me if ye can. There is a vairse in the Scripters, ye ken, that says 'Bear ye one another's burdens, and so fulfil the law of Christ.'"

" Truly, gudeman, but it's also said, 'Cast your burden on the Lord, and he will sustain you ; therefore if he lays the burden of others on us, we can lay them back on His loving heart, in the faith that He can bear the weight of both ; but ye may tell me what your burden is, and then I can judge whether I can help you or not."

" Weel, good woman, I am a brother o' Wattie Laidlaw's ; my name is Jamie Laidlaw ; I live at the Crosscleuch ; and my wife has ta'en in a bit orphan bairn to nurse. And with oor ain she is findin' her hands full ; so I am come to ask you to let me take your bit lassie that was wi' Katie Nicol at Hartleap, just to rock the cradle."

" Oh, man, but you make a heavy demand on me, and I cannot see my way to help you. My little Janet is but a bairn yet, and when at Hartleap she had been put to work above her strength, and she is just coming round again ; and I canna let her away, to be murdered outright before she is well into the world."

" Oh, woman, I am the faither o' a faimily ; my wife is a motherly woman ; and we fear and worship the God of Abraham. Do you think that we could ill-treat your bairn ? She shall fare like yin o' oor ain, she will get a lesson alang with them ; and as a faither I will train her while under my roof in the fear of the Lord ; and as for wages you must just trust us to do what's right. I cannot but say that I have an affection for Janet ; I saw something of her when I was ower at Hartleap helping to build their new house. Come away, my little woman, pit on your cap, and I will put my plaid roond you, and you will ride on the horse ahint me."

Without many more words, he draws Janet to him, wraps her in the plaid, and lifts her behind him on the horse. Janet's consent was never asked. She looked to her mother, observed the tear in her eye, and her heart melted as her mother said, " Farewell, Janet; God will take care of you."

The rest of the children are in great glee to see their sister on horseback—what a grand ride she will get! But who can describe the pangs of that young heart as she again leaves her happy home. She sighs, but she cannot cry. They ford the Yarrow, and make their way along the banks of St Mary's Loch. Janet's heart is sore. Will she always be like that lonely loch? Will she always be taken from those she loves! Is there to be no rest for her? Is she always to be sad and sorrowful? Poor Janet could not then see the Eye that was over her for good, and the unerring Hand that was leading her into green pastures and by still waters; but what she knows not now she will know hereafter. They pass Bowerhope, and Sandy Laidlaw congratulates Jamie on his success in getting Janet. He is acquainted with Janet's mother, knows she is a Christian woman, and remembers that the seed of the righteous is blessed. So he said—" Be kind to the lassie, Jamie, and He that blessed the Egyptian's house for Joseph's sake will give you a blessing with that bairn."

Jamie answered, " Amen."

The two arrive at Crosscleuch, and alight. Jamie

relates to his wife Tibbie's scruples at letting her lassie come to them, and his wife replies in a somewhat angry tone, " Does the wummin think we're haithens ? Did ye no tell her that we're Cameronians, and stick to the Covenants ? " Up to this time she has taken no notice of Janet, but now she gives her a little bread and milk and sets her to rock the cradle.

Jenny Burnet was the name of Janet's new mistress ; she was a tall, active, elderly woman, and had what was called in those days an "outward" temper. She spoke little, but when she did, it was mostly in an angry tone. She kept a clean house, however. There were three children. Jamie, a kind-hearted man, did not come short of his duty to Janet, so she soon felt more at home than she had done at Hartleap ; and God had in this place a very great blessing in store for her.

The other inhabitants of the place were farmer Walter Brydon, a very aged man, and his wife Peggy Grieve, with their family of four daughters and a son, all grown up. Other two daughters were from home—one married, the other in a situation. The four, with the son, at home were occupied on the farm, working in the fields. Jakeh, the youngest, was a shepherdess ; like Rachel of old, she kept her father's sheep. The Brydons were a really pious family, steadfast Cameronians, and faithful to all known duty. Family worship, night and morning, was observed in their house ; they had always a kind word and a homely welcome to strangers. All the members of this family took great interest in little Janet, and as she was often sent out in charge of the baby, she had many opportunities of mixing with them. In this she was encouraged by them, and not forbidden by the family whom she served.

Peggy Grieve, or rather "the gudewife," the name by which she was best known, was a pious woman, motherly and kind-hearted, and she took much interest in Janet's spiritual welfare. She promised her a sixpence if she learned all the *Single Questions* by heart. This was no great task, for Janet, as we have already seen, could repeat almost every one of them before she could read; and now that she was able to read pretty well she soon accomplished the task, and got the sixpence; and with a glad heart sent it to her mother.

Jakeh, the youngest daughter, was a God-fearing, warm-hearted young woman, and she and Janet drew naturally to each other. The love that bound these two hearts together might well be likened to that of David and Jonathan. Pleasantly and gratefully did little Janet drink in the love and affection of her new friend, and truly did she respond to it. All her little trials appeared as nothing when, with her infant charge wrapped in a shawl, she could wander up the burn-side and meet Jakeh, with her shepherdess plaid around her, followed by her two dogs, and often with a sickly lambkin in her arms; sometimes even with a dying ewe on her back. When they thus met, they would talk of Him who gathers the lambs with His arm and carries them in His bosom.

Jakeh would point out to Janet the glens and coverts where Cameron and other ministers preached to the poor persecuted flock. At the upper end of the loch was Riskenhope, where James Renwick preached one of his last sermons before he suffered martyrdom for God's cause and the Covenant. Here Janet learned lessons of heavenly wisdom, which she never forgot; and long after, when her locks were grey, she used to look back on these times with great gratitude and delight.

It would detain us too long to go into all the particulars of this term of Janet's service; but a calamity befell her there which may be recorded. In the autumn there had been a great thunderstorm, the Crosscleuch burn came down in high flood, and laid the potato field so much under water that all hands were at work lifting the potatoes, Janet among the rest. She came home wet to the skin, and, not having a change of clothes she was put to bed and her clothes hung to the fire to dry. Jamie awoke during the night, and felt the smell of burning. He found that the house was full of smoke, and on getting up he discovered that a little dog which they kept, and which had been lying between the chairs on which the clothes were, had upset one of them, and every stitch of clothing was burned to ashes. Poor Janet! her all was gone. Her mistress tucked up a petticoat of her own and tied a piece of an old shepherd's plaid about Janet's shoulders, and sent her home to Dryhope. Her mother did her best to provide other garments, and her girl returns to Crosscleuch without any needless delay.

When her engagement had expired it seemed to her like a few days in comparison with her stay at

Hartleap. On the day that she leaves, Jakeh accompanies her a mile on her way; and when they must part, they not only weep, but their wailing is heard at a distance. They pledge their love to God and each other while life lasts, and they part in the hope of meeting soon; but, alas! fifty long years had passed away ere they met again. That was for the first and last time at Ettrickside, on Thirlstane estate. Jakeh was then the worthy wife of Adam Glendinning. The fifty years had whitened the heads of both, but their hearts were young and warm as when they parted that summer day on the banks of St Mary's Loch.

> Bless'd be the tie that binds
>   Our hearts in Christian love;
> The fellowship of kindred minds
>   Is like to that above.

XII.

A Friendly Visit to Katie Nicol.

JANET is again at her father's fireside; she hands her mother her wages—ten shillings—with which she is well pleased, for though Janet got less money than at Hartleap she has gained in strength and cheerfulness. The bloom has returned to her cheek, and instead of the sad look and the involuntary sigh which used to crush her mother's heart, she has gained strength of body and is cheerful in spirit. She is in high spirits as she relates to her brothers and sisters her friendship with Jakeh, and tells about the spaining[1] of the lambs, the sheep marking, the clipping, the lambs following Jakeh into the house and sharing her porridge and milk.

'Robinson Crusoe' and 'Jack o' the Bean Stalk' fell into the shade while Janet related these wonders. Her father and mother were not less interested to hear that the two families had worship at the same hour morning and evening every day, and on Sabbath three times; the doors being always left open, so that if a stranger or a neighbouring shepherd were passing he might step in and join in the

---

[1] weaning.

exercises. This had been the practice since the days of the persecution.

Oh, what a happy night this is in the home at Dryhope! gladness fills every heart. After praise and prayer they lay them down to sleep, in the faith that the Lord makes them to dwell in safety.

Early next morning, Tibbie sets off for Selkirk to make some purchases, and she resolves that her little daughter shall have the full benefit of the wages she has earned. And truly Janet was not out of need, after the loss she had sustained at Crosscleuch. Among other useful articles her mother has bought a piece of tartan for a frock for her, her aunt at Selkirk has sent her a white caissered cap and tippet ; and when they are all turned out—oh, what riches! Janet thinks she will never want again.

After the frock is made, she expresses a wish to go to Hartleap and see Katie Nicol. Her mother is pleased at the thought, and she makes a pocket out of a piece of red cloth, and a pincushion, for Janet to take with her as a present to her old mistress. That day she is dressed in her new frock and white cap and tippet ; her shoes are brushed clean and blackened with soot from the girdle, her hair is flowing over her shoulders, and her heart is light. As she set out for Hartleap her mother remarked to her father that she was really a wonderful bairn.

Janet finds Katie all alone, and presents her gifts. The old woman is delighted; she claps her, takes her by the shoulders, turns her round, examines her from head to foot, and says, " Lassie, whae wad have thocht ye wad ever have been like that ? I can tell you we were a' gey mad when we heard that Jamie Laidlaw had ta'en ye away to Corsecleuch the very day Rob was gaun ower to ask ye to come back again; but Jennie, ye'll come back to us next summer, wull ye ? Eh, lassie ! how I have missed ye."

Katie hastened to set down a bowl of milk, cream and all, girdle scones, cheese, and butter, and pressed Janet to eat her fill. Then she took her to the byre to see the cow; she was sure " the cow would mind her; for bruit beasts," she said, " ken them that's kind to them, as weel as folk. Trusty," she says, "is deid now," and adds, " I believe it was naething but a broken hert he dee'd o' after ye gaed away. But ye'll come back, Jennie ? "

Janet held down her head and said nothing; but she must go and see the hens and the garden, the hay-stack, and the peat-stack. Katie does not know how kind to be, and when the time has come for Janet to leave for home, she gives her plenty of bread and butter, and a dad[1] of cheese, and accompanies her a long way on the road. When they were about to part, the old woman wept, and Janet wept, just out of sympathy with her. So they parted— never to meet again in this world; for not long after, Rob Shortreed went away to America, to push his fortune there, and took his mother with him. Janet had many thoughts about her old, first mistress, and the days she had lived with her at Hartleap; and she often wished she could have heard something of the poor old body, but no news ever reached

---

[1] a large piece.

her. A kindly feeling for Katie Nicol lingered long in her heart, and as she thought of her on the sea, she hoped that the wind did not blow a hurricane; for she had not forgotten the old woman's terror that night when the roof of the house at Hartleap had been blown off.

In returning from Hartleap on the day of her visit, and hurrying home to share her bread and cheese with her brothers and sisters, Janet is met by Willie and Nellie, giving her the news that Tibbie Hogg (an aunt of the Ettrick Shepherd) had arrived since she left. Tibbie was an old maid, and made her living by weaving tape, going from house to house and supplying the families with her handiwork, made of various widths from their own homespun thread. She was a very intelligent, pious woman; and therefore, not only for her work, but for her fellowship, she was always a welcome visitor. Janet had often sat by her mother while she was spinning the thread and Tibbie weaving the tape, listening to their conversation on heavenly things, and the news that Tibbie had arrived at Dryhope that day filled Janet with delight. But her joy, like all earthly joy, was short-lived; for at this time Tibbie's visit was not, as usual, to weave tape, but to inquire something concerning herself.

Peggie Hogg, a niece of Tibbie's, was married to William Brydon, a shepherd on the farm of Chapel-hope, and their house stood on the side of St Mary's Loch. In those days it bore the name of Summer-hope, but now a handsome hotel is built on the site where the cottage stood. Little Janet had gained a sort of popularity among the God-fearing people who in those days lived around the loch; and Tibbie Hogg's visit to Dryhope at this time was to engage her to go to Summerhope to rock the cradle and tend the cow. She is to get fifteen shillings for the half-year's service, and a lesson every day.

Why do I trouble the reader with such trifling incidents and details? Is it to raise Janet in their estimation, as if she had been something different from other children? This is not the aim of the writer, neither was it her experience even at this stage of her history. One day when hoeing the weeds in the garden, finding them too deep set for her slender arms to root up, she was overheard by a person unseen to exclaim, " O, my Father in heaven, these weeds are like the sins in my heart, they are ill to root up." Like all other children, Janet had a conscious feeling that she did not always say or do what was right in the sight of God, but in after years God's care over the meanest thing in life was seen by her more enlightened eyes. In relating the smallest incidents in her own life, she gives glory to God for all the way in which He led her; and it would be a great satisfaction to her if this imperfect relation of her story leads any of her young friends to put their trust in God, and mark all His tender care over them.

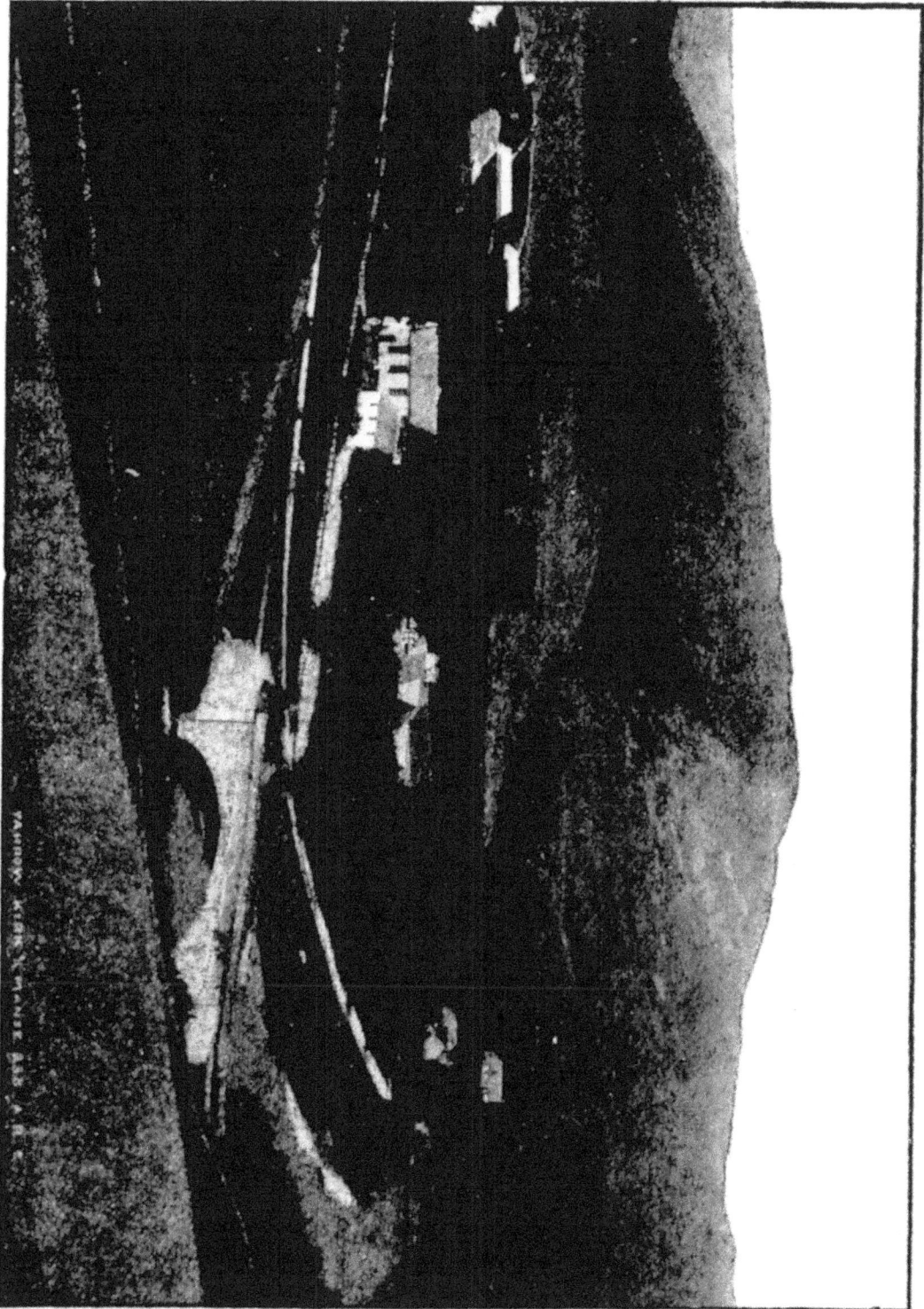

Yarrow Kirk and Surrounding Scenery.

XIII.

A Third Call to Service.

AS the outcome of Tibbie Hogg's visit, Janet has to go back to Summerhope. She feels sorry to leave her home again, yet the trial is not so great as on former occasions. She had made the acquaintance of the people at Summerhope while she was at Crosscleuch, and had rather liked them. On the night before leaving, her father, after worship, gives her good counsel. Her mother reminds her that God's eye is ever looking into her heart. She must not forget her prayers, and she must remember the Sabbath day to keep it holy—not thinking her own thoughts, nor speaking her own words, nor doing her own works on that holy day; for God had given it as a sign or pledge of the holy rest that, notwithstanding the fall of man, yet remains for those that love and obey Him. And she tells her that because Jesus loved righteousness and hated all iniquity, God raised Him from the dead on the Sabbath morning, and took Him up to heaven to take possession of the heavenly home for all that would follow in His steps.

After Janet and her brothers and sisters had

gone to bed, her mother set about packing up her few articles of clothing; for Janet is to start early in the morning. The mother is pleased as she ties up the little bundle, containing, as it does, many comfortable articles of clothing, and she remarks to the father, " No one can mock my little Janet with her bare back this time; her mother has made her clean and hale without; may God make her pure within ! "

" They are all God's gifts, gudewife. Let us thank the Giver, not only for her clothes but for herself; she is a precious gift from God himself; may she grow up like a lily in His garden, watered every moment by His hand, guided by His eye, which marks even the sparrow's fall ! "

The clothes which Janet is to wear next day are all laid out on a chair, her little bundle is put beside them, and then father and mother retire to rest. To the labouring man sleep is sweet, and he yields himself up to quiet rest, without fear of thief or robber entering his humble dwelling, as there is nothing to tempt to covetousness. Yet, while here in the valley of conflict, God has many ways of trying his faith. The whole family are at rest, every eye sealed in quiet repose; but towards morning the parents are startled by a cry of alarm from one of the boys. The father awakes, starts from his bed, and is astonished to find the house full of smoke, and something blazing in the middle of the floor. The doors and windows are thrown open, and to the surprise and sorrow of the parents they find the chair on which Janet's clothes had lain almost consumed to ashes, and again every stitch of the clothing burned—all gone but her shoes. It was never known how this sad occurrence happened. Poor Tibbie can scarcely refrain from a sort of wail of despair— "Oh, what shall I do with my poor bairn? She has a hard beginning; what her latter end will be, God only knows!"

"Yes, gudewife, we can leave her in His hands, and it becomes us to put our hands on our mouth and be dumb before Him, because He hath done it! We may say like Job, 'Shall we receive good at the hand of the Lord and shall we not receive evil?' Let us wait on Him; He can yet make the dark clouds to break with blessings on our head. We have sinned; but while we deserved wrath, He has remembered mercy. Let us praise Him for sparing us all alive, so that we have not awaked in the blackness of darkness. Sad as we feel this morning, it is not the torment of the worm that never dieth nor the fire that is not quenched." While John is seeking to soothe his poor wife he feels the load on his own heart growing lighter.

We now see Janet in her tenth year, leaving her father's house, for service, for the third time. She takes very short steps, and often looks back towards the home she has left. She is clothed with some of her sisters' old things, which are not at all a good fit, and these give her the look of a little old woman. Those who saw her in her tartan frock and white tippet and cap on the previous morning would scarcely have recognised her as the same little blooming daisy; but whatever she felt on this score, no murmur escapes her lips; her mind is occupied with other thoughts. Her father is leaving Dryhope at the Whitsunday term, and going to Fernielea, on Tweedside, four miles from Selkirk. There is a school there, and Janet is to go home at Martinmas, to be there in the winter and attend the school with her brothers and sisters. Her sister Bella, who accompanies her to Summerhope, is cheering her by saying that when she comes home with her fifteen shillings she will get another new frock.

They arrive at Summerhope, and get a kindly welcome from Peggy Hogg. Bella tells about the burning of Janet's clothes, and explains that her mother will try and send something as soon as possible. But Peggy is so pleased to have Janet that she promises to supply her need of anything in that direction. She is allowed to see her sister a little way on her home-going, and the parting was a sorrowful one for both. Bella, some years older than Janet, had never been in good health, and had always a look of sadness; and Janet's tenderness to her suffering sister had drawn them very close to each other. They had often talked of death and eternal things, and had sometimes retired to the hill-side and prayed together. Now they part: Janet goes back to Summerhope, Bella homewards; and God has His eye on them both.

Janet is much pleased with the surroundings of her new abode. The house stands on a high bank, commanding a view of the loch from head to foot, and is also in the centre of a large garden, terraced in front of the house, and surrounded with a dry-stone dyke. At the top is a row of mountain ash trees, which separate the garden from the public road. This flat part is planted with cabbages, peas, beans, greens, and leeks ; and in a border in front of the window are several kinds of flowers—sweetwilliam, daisies, pansies, southernwood, peppermint, and camomile. That was an indispensable plant in those quarters, and much used as medicine. At the back of the house a considerable break of ground ran down the bank near to the edge of the loch, which is separated from it by a few old ash and beech trees. On this plot are planted potatoes and turnips, and a considerable space is sown with barley. The whole is surrounded with a fale dyke,[1] over which the sheep often make their way, so that they require no little watching by the inmates.

The house is of somewhat modern construction, and has two apartments. In the one lives Willie Brydon's mother, a very respectable, intelligent old woman, who acts as midwife in the surrounding district ; in the other we find Willie, who is the shepherd, his young wife Peggie Hogg (a cousin of the Ettrick Shepherd), and their little son Willie. The furniture is all new, the walls are white-washed, a window to the back commands a view of the loch and surrounding hills, and so takes in Bowerhope, Dryhope, Kirkstead, and Cappercleuch. Close in a corner stands the cradle, where little Jenny sat many lonely hours rocking her infant charge, with the door locked on her — the while Peggie and her mother-in-law, Nellie Bald, are a mile away among

---

[1] A wall built of turf.

the hills, working on the peats for the winter's fuel.

But the duties which Janet is called to perform here are easy compared with what she had to do at Hartleap ; she is never asked to do anything beyond her strength. She is kindly treated, and gets a lesson every day. She sees or hears nothing amiss. There is family worship night and morning, the door at such seasons being always set open, as was done at Crosscleuch, so that any stranger or shepherd passing at the time may find his way in to join in the worship. And though there is no closet to which Janet may retire and say her prayers, yet she remembers an observation of old Elspeth Laidlaw at Yarrowford, "that a praying heart gets aye a praying place." So she finds one in a corner of the byre ; and there she says her prayers. She has not yet really learned to pray, to hold communion with God in the secret chamber of the heart ; but she is true to what she does know, and night and morning she repeats her prayers, and goes to her daily work with a light heart. The keeping of the Sabbath is still a heavy task to her ; she fears lest she profane the holy day, and its return makes her unhappy.

Her first duty every morning, the Sabbath not excepted, was to drive the cow to a little park about a quarter of a mile from the house. In fear of thinking her own thoughts on this holy day, she commences to repeat the 'Single Questions,' including the Lord's Prayer, the graces and creed at the end of the book ; also texts of Scripture, and psalms and hymns, all the way to the park and back, and all the day; and when she has gone over all she could remember, begins again with the 'Questions.'

Do her nieces smile at her ignorance? Be it so. What she knew, or did not know, she had at least learned that there was a holy God, who could see into the dark corners of her heart, and one day would require from her and all men an account of the deeds done in the body; and she wished to please Him and be at peace with Him. If any judge her wrongly, let them sit at Luther's feet; he was a learned man, and he will explain to them the secret of Janet's fear to offend God.

It is a great relief to Janet in trying to keep the Sabbath holy to be asked by Peggie to bring her Bible and get a lesson; and Peggie in her way tries to instruct her in the fear of the Lord. Perhaps the one had not much more knowledge than the other; but what knowledge Peggie had, she tries to communicate to her little maid, and one day she said to her, " Janet, I will give you a sixpence if you will commit to memory the fifty-third chapter of Isaiah. I think it must be the best chapter in the Bible, for I never mind of hearing a minister preach but he had a bit of it either in his sermon or his prayer."

Janet did commit to memory next day that blessed portion of God's word, but many a time, like the Ethiopian, did she wonder of whom the prophet spoke; but in after years she found that it referred to Him who was the source of all her joy—Jesus, the altogether lovely, the chiefest among ten thousand. All her life she has felt deeply indebted to Peggie for her motherly care and kindness.

XIV.

A First Attempt at Letter-Writing.

A LITTLE burn takes its rise at the top of the hill that overlooks the lonely, humble shepherd's cot. By many crooked turns it falls over a rock, forming a little cascade, which had worn out a deep pool at the end of the house; then winding its way by the side of the garden the streamlet terminates its little course by falling into the loch. A little above the public road in a bend of the burn is a little table-land, where the clothes were bleached.

One morning, while Peggy is milking the cow, Janet carries the linen web, which has just come home from the weaver, to the table-land, and spreads it out to bleach. She gets early to bed here, and as she rises feels rested and refreshed, and she is able, in her little way, to drink in the beauty of the scenery around her. The sun has risen and gilded the tops of the hills with its golden beams. On the lovely green slopes are flocks of sheep, and the shepherds with their dogs are moving among them. All are mirrored in the loch, which in the calm of this summer morning is like a sheet of glass. The stillness around is broken only by the bleating of the lambs, the bark of the shepherds' dogs, the cry of the muircock, and the quacking of the wild ducks on the loch. Janet thinks that heaven must be something like this, yet she feels a sadness at her heart. Oh, if only her father, mother, sisters, and brothers were here, she would ask no other heaven; so, with these thoughts in her mind, she sometimes weeps, and sometimes sings part of that lovely hymn—

> There is a land of pure delight
> Where saints immortal reign,
> Infinite day excludes the night,
> And pleasures banish pain.

Another duty that devolved on Janet was to watch the sheep from climbing the fale dyke and helping themselves to the produce of the garden, so she and the old dog " Yarrow " were kept in constant exercise during the early part of the day. Janet was sometimes put to grief, however, by old " Yarrow " driving the sheep into the garden instead of driving them out. The poor old dog was both nearly blind and deaf, but he had done good service in his day, and was not only a favourite with the family, but much thought of by all the neighbours on account of his wisdom and sagacity in other days. Once, Sandy Laidlaw, of Bowerhope, was lost among the snow, and after three days of unsuccessful search, old " Yarrow " scented him out under an avalanche of snow which had fallen from the top of Bowerhope Law to the edge of the loch. Sandy was alive, but much exhausted, when help came to him. He never forgot his deliverer, and during the life of the old dog, he paid an annual visit to Summerhope and presented him with a lamb's leg.

A little way from the house, on the upper side of the public road, there was a very large whinstone, which was known by the name of "the greystone," and was often spoken of as a trysting-place. One would often hear it said, " I will meet you at 'the greystone,'" or, " It is so many miles to 'the greystone.'" Here we often find Janet with her little shepherd's plaid around her, with old " Yarrow " at her feet, sitting throughout the long summer's day watching the sheep. Many a longing look she casts down the Yarrow to the hills beyond which her father and mother are now living, and many a sigh she gives as she counts the weeks when, with her fifteen shillings, she will take the road for Fernielea, and once more be at home.

Peggie Hogg had taught Janet what was called the "sampler stitch," and one day she gave her a piece of thin green cloth and some yellow silk thread, and told her to try and sew something on it, thinking that it would keep her from wearying when attending to her duties outside. One day she sat on "the greystone," musing on what she would sew on the bit of cloth, when the idea struck her that she would try to sew a map of the loch and its surroundings, and send it home. How delighted, she thought, they would be with it.

The view from where she sat was much lovelier than that taken in from Dryhope, and Janet sets to work, heart and hand, though she knew just as much about maps as the man in the moon. Why then does she entertain her nieces with the story of a bit green cloth and a little yellow thread? Well, it is just that they may mark the leading of God's providence, and see how he can out of little things bring great results. This little bit of green cloth and yellow thread had a great deal to do with Janet's history through all her after life.

At the time, it beguiled many lonely hours; and when at last it is finished, she thinks further about sending it home. But will they understand it? Oh, that she could get away for a while; she would run all the road to Fernielea and explain it to the loved ones there, and then run back. But who would watch the sheep whilst she was away? No, no, Janet cannot ask away. Then how she wishes that she had learned to write, for then she could have written a long letter and explained all about her green map.

A letter that her father had written to Willie Brydon, her employer, to inquire after his little daughter, she always carried in her pocket; she had managed to trace out the words in an imperfect way, and many, many times had she read it over. She takes it out of her pocket and reads it for the twentieth time or more. She considers the letters, and thinks she could copy them, but then she has neither paper, pen, nor ink; and more than that, though she could make out the sense of her father's writing, there were some of the letters she was not very sure about. For instance, she could not distinguish very well E from F. At last she notices that there is a little bit of blank paper on her father's letter, This she cuts off, takes out the Question book, looks carefully how the letters in it are formed, then takes a pin, and on the blank piece of paper pricks with the point of the pin their form, and thus " writes " a letter to her father. But the space on her paper was very limited, and therefore soon filled up; all she has room for is the following—

" *My dear father and mother I am well thank God Peggie is kind to me I hope you are all well God bless you Your daughter Janet* "

So she ties up the letter and her green map in a bit of rag, and gives it to Robin Hogg, the carrier. There is no address upon it, but she tells him to hand it in to Jamie Cumming, the baker at Selkirk. He is an old acquaintance of her father's, and he will get it on Sabbath, as he always calls on Jamie between sermons.

One other little incident out of many that were helpful to Janet's faith and hope in after years may be mentioned here. It is a calm summer's morning, and the sun shining on the drops of dew made the hill look like a bank of silvery pearls. Janet had often thought when the sun shone on the loch that it would be like the golden streets of heaven that her mother used to tell her about. Would the hills there be like silver? Oh, to be there, with father, mother, sisters, and brothers, never more to part! But death and the judgment day had to be passed through, and, oh! she thinks if she is not one of the elect, she will be separated from her parents for ever. Oh, if God would tell her that she is one of the elected number, how she would love Him! These and many other things she pondered over in her mind as she sat on "the greystone" watching the sheep, her only companion being old blind and deaf "Yarrow," and as he licks her hand and fawns upon her, Janet fondly claps the old dog.

While she is thus musing she sees something of unusual size rise from the opposite hill and soar high in the air. It is not a crow, or any bird she had ever seen, but whatever it is, it is coming in a direct line to where she sits. Is it an angel sent from God to take her away, or is it an evil spirit to carry her to the blackness of darkness for having had hard thoughts of God for making death the wages of sin? She is terror-struck; she trembles as she sees the large grey figure approach her high up in the air, and yet it appears not to move a wing. At last as it passes over her head she hears a soft, soughing sound, and ventures to look up. The figure appears as if it was resting in the air. At length it passes over her, and alights on a high rock which overhangs the loch; but only for a few minutes; then it rises, wings its way through the air, and disappears.

Janet's mind is relieved when the shepherd comes in for dinner, and asks if any of them had seen the old eagle flying about, seeking for its prey. At one time eagles were no strangers in that quarter; they used to carry away lambs, and the shepherds had declared war against them, and they were now seldom seen. This one appeared to pay a yearly visit to the place, but was watched so closely that it seldom got any prey. Janet in after years often thanked God that she had had an opportunity of seeing an eagle, as it helped her to understand better than she could otherwise have done the Scriptures where the eagle is spoken of; and often she used to sing that hymn,

"On eagles' wings they mount, they soar,
Their wings are faith and love."

But the autumn has come round. Janet has had her share in gathering in the precious fruits of the earth and helping to store them up for winter; and now the end of her term of service is drawing nigh; her heart is light, for she is going home, and then to the school. She was told she had given great satisfaction to Willie and Peggie by her quiet, biddable manner; and as they are loth to part with her, Willie writes to her father that he wishes her to remain all winter. It had been a very late harvest, and meal, as well as everything else, was dear. Her father's wages were less than when he was at Dryhope, and there was a large family to provide for. In these circumstances he and her mother might have been persuaded to let her remain, but Janet's parcel containing her green map and letter had reached their destination; and, as she has already said, that had a great deal to do with shaping her future history. Her father and mother had been much puzzled to make out the meaning of these two obscure documents, but one day two of the Misses Pringle, of Yair, step in. This is not their first friendly visit. They had learned from Janet's mother something of their little daughter at service at St Mary's Loch, and of her hard beginning, as her mother used to describe it. The ladies are shown Janet's parcel, and the piece of paper that her parents thought she had been trying to make some flowers upon; but Miss Susan discovers that the dotted parts are letters of the alphabet, and after a little study she makes out and reads Janet's letter, to their surprise and joy. The young lady asks permission to take the map and letter with her, that she might show them to her father and mother; and in the meantime they press John and Tibbie to bring Janet home and put her to the school. John therefore writes to Willie Brydon that there's not to be two ways of it—Janet is to come home at the term, and go to school. This is one result of Janet's first letter, but it is destined to have other effects in days to come.

May her nieces learn from this trifling incident that while there is nothing too great for the grasp of the Almighty God, there is also nothing too small for His notice; and that the very hairs of our heads are numbered!

XV.

A First Lesson in Manners.

HE term day has come at length. Janet has got her breakfast of porridge and milk. She goes to the byre to clap the cow and bid her farewell, and in her little dark corner she says her prayers. She is dressed in a yellow and brown skirt, made up from an old petticoat of Peggie's, and a blue jacket made from an old coat of Willie's; but, though not braw, she is tidy and clean. Pieces of bread and cheese are in her pocket, and fifteen shillings in her handkerchief. This is placed in her bosom, and Peggie pins it to her stays, lest she lose it by the way.

With her bundle, which is neither large nor heavy, she sets out thus, in her tenth year, to walk from Summerhope to Fernielea, a distance of at least twenty miles. Peggie, her mistress, and little Willie are to accompany her to Megget-foot, and Janet has the boy in her arms. Peggie bids her farewell, then sees her wade the stream—for there was no bridge over the Megget then—they wave each other adieu, not without tears on both sides. Where the population was so small as it was then around St Mary's Loch, friendships were easier formed and longer retained than in places more crowded. Thus, while Janet is going on her way rejoicing at the prospect of again being at home, there is sorrow in her heart, the pain of parting with Peggie, for she had been kind to her. Poor little Janet, like all others, has to learn that this seeming contradiction must follow her all through her pilgrimage on earth.

She walks, sometimes runs, down the vale, and at length she comes to " the dowie dens." She remembers the flitting to Dryhope, and much that happened on the road that day, but her mind is more taken up with the thought of meeting loved ones at home. Her sister Bella meets her at the Raelees, not far from Fernielea ; takes her little bundle, puts her arm round Janet's waist and supports her a little, for she is now footsore and very weary after such a long journey. But she is soon at home, and joyfully lays her fifteen shillings in her mother's lap ; then she parts her bread and cheese among her brothers and sisters, for though very hungry, she could not think of eating it, as she had nothing else to give them.

In passing Philiphaugh Mill—the old corn mill which then stood near the road-side a little above Beechwood—she had rapped at a door and asked for a drink of water. The woman, seeing her a stranger, asked how far she had come, and, perceiving no doubt Janet's motive for asking a drink, gave her a piece of bread, which she ate heartily, and her eyes were brightened, for by this time she was feeling faint. Her parents were pained at the thought of her long fast, yet they were pleased with her unselfish love.

Next evening Janet is well rested, and as they sit around the fire, she is interesting her brothers and sisters by relating her experience and adventures on the side of St Mary's Loch. The parents are delighted to see the interchange of love among their offspring. It is drawing near the hour for worship, and the father, looking round his happy family, says —" Bairns, listen to me a few minutes before you join in the worship of the great God that made heaven and earth. My children, my beloved children, your father loves you with an intensity that can only be understood by a Christian parent. Oh, my children, I believe, as regards this world's goods, I am the poorest man in the parish ; I am not sure if your thrifty mother will find as much meal as will fill your mouths on the coming morning ; but as regards love, the love of my children, I think I am the wealthiest man in the world—yes, wealthier than King George. God has given me the gift of nine children—one whose precious dust lies in Selkirk kirkyaird, whose spirit is before the throne of God. His mission on earth was a short one ; it was just as it were a little silver thread let down from God, and recalled, just to draw us up to the father of our spirits, the fountain of love. But I can look around on your happy faces this night and count eight, and it is no little comfort to me, nor less glory to God, that I can witness before Him that hitherto I never had a grieved heart with any one of you ; you have returned my love, and my cup is full. But, my children, we, in the purpose of God, are not to live here always; your father, according to the course of nature, must soon go the way of all the earth; but what comfort to my heart is the thought that you will not be orphans. Your Father in heaven is, and will be, a better father to you than I ever can be. He is love, He is the father of your spirits; return His love by walking in righteousness, in wisdom's ways, which are ways of pleasantness, and whose paths are peace. The young lions may be hungry and may lack their food, but they that wait on the Lord shall not want any good thing. But, oh, my children, remember that Wisdom says, ' If ye set at nought my counsels, and will have none of my reproofs, I also will laugh at your calamity, and mock when your fear cometh.' Now, my children, let us worship the one true God, by lifting up our hearts with our hands to Him, our Father in heaven, asking that He would hold up our goings, so that our footsteps slide not.

> Oh, what a pleasant sight to see
> A loving household worship Thee!
> At once they sing, at once they pray,
> They hear of heaven, and learn the way.

Is it not a little heaven below? Who would not like to join them rather than mix with fools, whose laughter is like the crackling of thorns under a pot, which passes away in smoke?

On the Monday following Janet's arrival she enters the school. Mr Park, the schoolmaster,

H

finds Janet a tolerably good reader, and she is put into a class of boys and girls somewhat in advance of her in years and also in knowledge, but none are more attentive to their lessons. On the Saturday they have each to repeat a question out of the 'Shorter Catechism,' also each get a portion from a psalm to learn on the coming Sabbath, which they are to repeat on Monday morning ere they commence their lessons. In those days there were no Sabbath-schools in the district.

The Misses Pringle, of Yair, learn that Janet has arrived home, and gone to school; they hasten to pay her mother a visit, and see what they consider must be " a curiosity of a bit lassie." The letter and the green map are produced, and Janet explains all the wonders around the loch which she had attempted to sew on her bit green cloth with the yellow silk thread. The ladies are amused with her ingenuity, and they propose that after school hours she shall go to Yair house for an hour every day, and one of the ladies will teach her to sew.

In the meantime Mrs Pringle sends a message, saying she would like to see the wee servant lassie. In compliance with the wish, Janet is dressed neat and clean in her skirt, blue jacket, and white pinafore; her mother directs her to go to the kitchen door, but the ladies are on the lookout for her; and as she approaches, they throw up the dining room window and call her to come round by the front door, where Miss Susan receives her and ushers her into the dining room. Mrs Pringle welcomes her, and directs her to make a curtsey. Janet is bewildered; she has now for the first time seen a carpet, and is afraid to set her foot on it, for she wonders why such a fine thing should be walked on. Many questions are asked of her, which she modestly answers, looking all the time down to the carpet, with her finger in her mouth. Mrs Pringle tells her that when she speaks to any one, especially ladies, she must look them straight in the face, take her finger from her mouth, and fold her hands, and stand erect. Janet thought this would not be a becoming position for her, and she feels shame, but musters courage and promptly obeys. Mrs Pringle gives her some good counsel, telling her that a good character is better than fine clothes or money, and she places a shilling in Janet's hand, and tells her to say " Thank you, ma'am," and then make her curtsey. The young ladies lead her to the door, and tell her to come back at a certain hour every day, and they will teach her to sew. Janet is bewildered by this first visit and the new ways and the new things she has seen. She cannot make out the use of many of them. Why is the window hung with crimson drapery? What was that box or press in the corner that the youngest lady was playing on, something like a fiddle? Above all, why were ladies so plainly dressed; and why their bare bosoms and bare arms? All is mysterious! but for all she saw, she feels her own home the happier. She has seen for the first time something of the ways of people in higher life, she has got her first lesson in manners, and has experienced kindness from those above her — all being another harvest of fruit from her green map.

Janet, now in her humble happy home, is getting better acquainted with God, and the more she knows of Him, the more she sees her own shortcomings. When she left Summerhope, Peggie threw out some hints about her coming back; but Janet looks to remaining at home for the winter, and thinks she will have learned to be very good before it ends. She gets the 'Annals of the Poor' from Miss Susan Pringle, and her thirsty soul drinks in the story of 'The Young Cottager.' Oh, to know Jesus as little Jane knew Him.

When she could do so unobserved, she would run to a dyke side or among the trees, and fall on her knees and cry out, "Lord Jesus, remember me, now that thou art in Thy kingdom!" and when at any time she was betrayed into foolish sports with other children, she would feel ashamed for wasting time. It might be said of her that, as she grew in knowledge, she grew in favour with rich and poor, and was, perhaps, on the brink of being spoiled. But the eye of God is upon her—He who appoints the bounds of our habitation, whose unerring wisdom is best fitted to lead us to seek after Him, though he is not far from any one of us. Yes, her unseen Heavenly Father is thinking and planning for little Janet. She has further lessons of heavenly wisdom to learn, and the hardest and most important is, that the pride of our fallen nature makes it needful for us to give up our own selfish wills for His glory and the good of others.

Six happy weeks Janet has spent in her happy home ; she is attentive to her lessons, and also helpful to her mother. A little sister had been born into the family before Janet came home, and she has in some measure taken the place of her little brother Robert. Janet takes her out, and betimes rocks the cradle ; and while she learns her lessons she also sings—

We may, like the ships, on tempests be tossed,
On perilous deeps, but cannot be lost ;
Though Satan enrages the wind and the tide,
The promise assures us, the Lord will provide.

XVI.

The Troubles of Lambing Time.

OWARDS the end of the year, one cold bleak day, Janet is thus employed, and lifting her eyes she sees to her surprise the old white horse on which she rode behind Jamie Laidlaw to Crosscleuch. On its back sits Peggy Grieve, the gudewife of Crosscleugh. She had come to visit a married daughter at Yair farm, and was also commissioned to plead the cause of Willie and Peggie Brydon with Janet's parents, that she might go back to them at Summerhope. They think Janet is indispensable to Peggie's comfort. Her parents may name any wages, and Peggie Grieve will give her a ride behind her when she returns, in the course of three days. Oh, the pangs that wring little Janet's heart. Are all her hopes to be blasted, as it were in one day? Shall she ever be like Noah's dove, never find rest for the sole of her foot? Shall she be like Cain, wandering up and down on the earth? No, dear child, no rest —not that God grudges you that, but because of His plan. He is training you for an inheritance, incorruptible, and undefiled, and that fadeth not away.

Janet slips to the closet, and there she weeps, and prays that God would allow her to remain at home; yet her heart melts when she thinks of Peggie, and she makes up her mind to go if her mother says she ought. Poor Tibbie, she has a large family, and times are bad; so she consents to the entreaties of the Brydons. Janet says, " Mother, do not be sorry, I am willing to go."

The three days passed quickly by, and on the day appointed Peggie Grieve, with the old white horse, calls for Janet. Over the horse's back is hung a wallet, into which Janet's little articles are put. It is a sort of saddle, called "soods," on which the good woman sits, and with Janet behind her they start on their long journey. The parting again of Janet with her sisters, brothers, father, and mother, was a very trying one, but we must draw a veil over it, for words of ours would fail to describe the sorrowful event.

When our travellers reached Yarrowford they halted, staying a little with Elspeth Laidlaw, and they were refreshed by their Christian fellowship with the old woman. In this cold, short, winter day it is getting dark when they reach Summerhope; Janet alights, and the gudewife and the old white horse make their way to Crosscleuch.

Janet gets a warm welcome from her old friends at Summerhope. Peggie can easily see from her bleared eyes that her heart is sore, and she does all in her power to comfort her. She presents her with a pair of new clogs that Willie had bought for her at Moffat fair, a blue flannel petticoat, and a neat little shift from the linen web which she had bleached during the summer, and also a red-cheeked apple. Janet is much pleased with all her presents, but such a bonnie red-cheeked apple, how can she eat it alone? Could she not keep it and part it with her brother Robert and little Nellie? Janet, along with the rest of the family, had been taught by their mother always to give to each other a share of what they got, aiming thus to wean them from the root of evil, a selfish nature, and also to teach them as brothers and sisters to bear one another's burdens. This custom, even of dividing a peppermint drop, made it sore for her to eat the apple alone; but it will not keep a whole year, and she gives little Willie the half of it.

She claps and sleeks old "Yarrow," and must go to the byre to do the same with the cow. In a shepherd's house these animals are considered as part of the family. Janet takes, as she used to do in former days, the potato peelings to the cow, and thinks she knows her. But she had also another errand to the byre, and she goes into the dark corner and says her prayers.

After a supper of good porridge and milk, and as she looks wearied, Peggie tells her she may go to bed, and that she may lie in the morning as long as she likes. She retires to rest, but, oh! the bed seems empty; no little brother with his arms around her neck, no sister Nellie at her back; no mother to tuck in the blankets and place a kiss on her cheek, and bid her say her hymns. Amid her loneliness she cries herself to sleep.

We pass over the rest of Janet's life this year at Summerhope, as it would be almost a repetition of what has already been given. Only one thing, which was then omitted, must be now stated. To the shepherds in those quarters, the lambing time is the most anxious period of the year, especially if the season should be a wet one. Janet has her share both in the anxiety and toil. We see her up in a cold, wet, spring morning, her petticoats tucked up with her garters, her plaid around her shoulders, climbing the hill appointed to her by Willie. She carries a pitcher of warm milk, and lays hold upon any little trembling lamb that lies in her way. Having been taught the art of feeding such feeble ones by Willie, she pours from her own mouth the warm milk into the mouth of the little helpless creature. It may be that she finds the mother ewe dead; in that case she takes off her plaid, ties the little orphan lamb in it, and gets it on her back. After hours of such wearying toil, she returns home wet and worn out, with sometimes two lambs on her back and one in her arms. Then she lays them around the good peat fire, and rubs them gently, giving them more warm milk. When they are sufficiently revived, she takes them to the byre, where accommodation has been provided in anticipation of these events. Here Janet attends to their wants; she gives to each a name by which she calls them; and long after they have been sent out to the green hill-side to shift for themselves, when she calls them by name they will run to her and share in her forenoon "piece;" and sometimes they will follow her into the house, which, however, is now felt to be an annoyance to the inmates.

There is no Sabbath-school, and no church near to which she might go, yet she thinks much of Him who is the Good Shepherd, who carries the lambs in His arms, and she learns to love Him ; and from her observation of the shepherds around her, she understands how gently He leads those that are with young. Thus God is training Janet, and she is drinking in lessons of heavenly wisdom, although when sitting on "the greystone," and far from her father's house, she sometimes feels her lot to be a hard one; yet under God's eye it proves otherwise. She had been carried far from the vanity of a giddy world, and placed where she learned a Saviour's love. Thus she sits and sings, "The Lord is my Shepherd," not by rote, but with love in her heart, for she has profited from the lessons learned from her daily occupation among the lambs.

The expected little stranger had come to the home at Summerhope in the gift of a little daughter. The winter was a very severe one, and St Mary's Loch was frozen over. This made the way shorter for the neighbours on the opposite side, and the shepherds' wives could cross the ice to pay their visit to Peggie and present their gifts. Nor did they forget little Janet, the little stranger in their midst —be this recorded to their honour. Whether it was done in obedience to divine precept or from kindly feeling, they fulfilled the apostle's injunction, "Be not forgetful to entertain strangers; " and no doubt they had their reward.

The winter and the spring passed cheerily by, and summer, with its toils and pleasures and profits, is also drawing to a close. Janet is looking forward to returning to her father's house once more. By this time he had removed to a better situation near Peebles, her eldest sisters and brothers are all in good places, doing for themselves; and the parents look hopefully forward to Janet's return. They had learned that Lady Hay, of Kingsmeadows, had opened a school at Peebles, for teaching little girls reading, writing, and sewing; the fees are moderate, and they make up their minds that when Janet comes home she shall be sent to this school; for they are anxious that she should now have a little rest from hard toil, and get more learning.

The days fled swiftly past, and the November term has come round. Janet is again leaving Summerhope, not without deep regrets, as before, on Peggie's part. But she is going home to attend school, and to stay there for a long time. Her bundle is a little larger than it was before, and her presents make it heavier; and she has got thirty shillings for her winter and summer wages. Oh, how rich she feels! What will her mother say when she lays all these shillings in her lap?

Peggie and the bairns again accompany Janet to Megget-foot, and see her safe on the other side of the stream. The parting had been again a sad one on both sides, but had they known that they were never to meet again in this world, it would have been more solemn. Sufficient, however, to the day is the evil thereof; God saves us all the pain He can, and lays not on us more than we can bear. Willie and Peggie Brydon with their family shortly after this went to America.

Janet has another weary travel, but gets home in safety. She gives her wages to mother, divides her spoil with the little ones, and is delighted with the prospect of going to school. Her mother buys her a new frock with money of her own earning, and in the following week she enters Lady Hay's school. There, by her attention to her lessons, she is not long in gaining the kindly notice of the superinten- dent — Mrs Johnston, a widow lady of kindly dis- position, but very delicate in health. Two weeks after Janet has gone to the school the teacher is unable to continue at her duties; she is confined to her bed; and her mother, an aged lady, takes her place. A month later Mrs Johnston dies, the seminary is closed; and here end Janet's school days.

If book learning were to be necessary to fit one for heaven, Janet thinks she has little chance to get there. She is therefore somewhat sad, for she has not as yet learned that she has a Teacher nearer her than any earthly one, and One who cannot die; and that if she yields to His voice in the inner cham- ber of her heart, He will lead her to green pastures and by still waters. Let us follow her a little further on her journey through the wilderness of this world, and also mark the guiding hand of God, that we, with her in after days, may give Him all the glory for both the good and the ill by which he was edu- cating her.

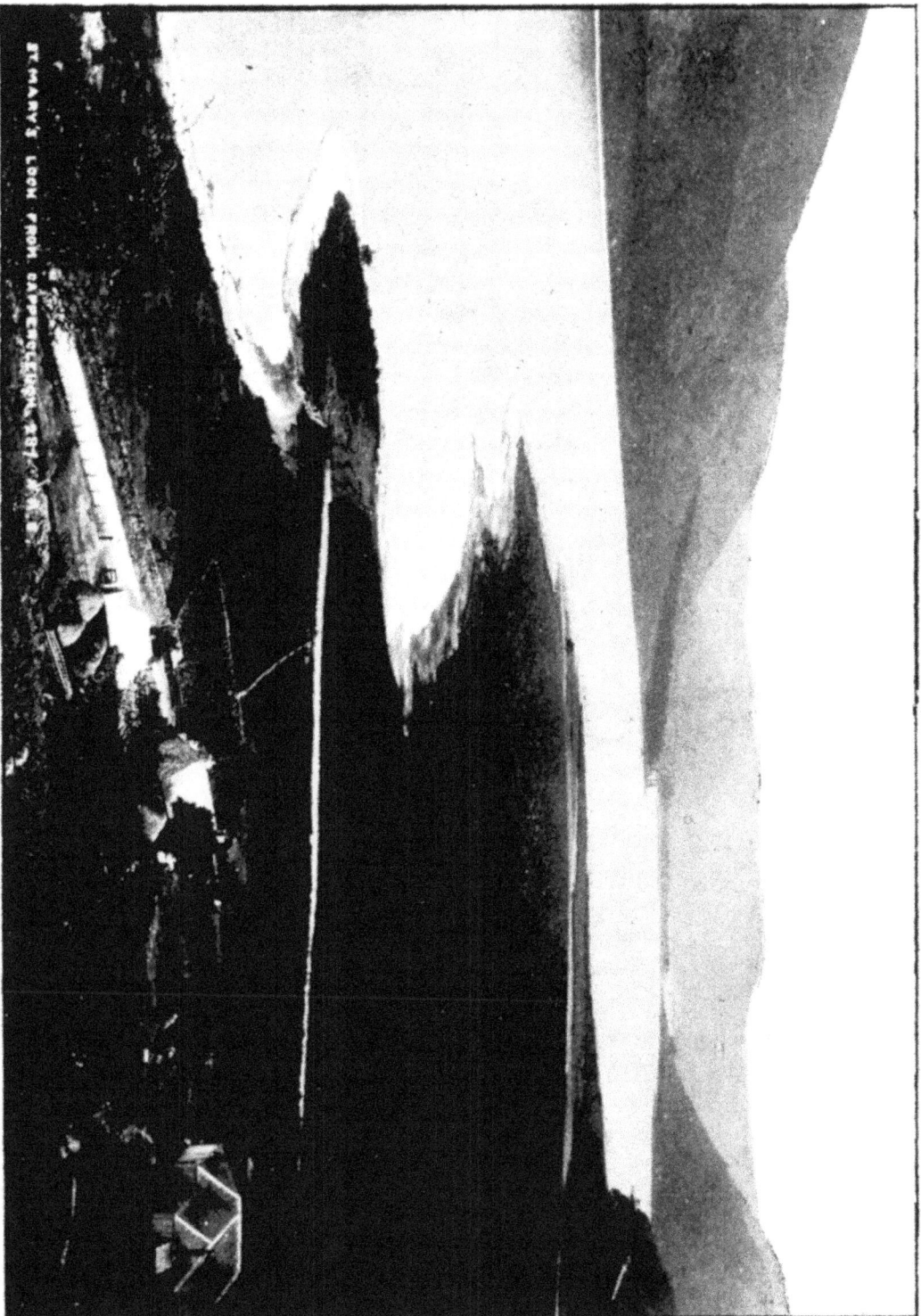

St Mary's Loch.

XVII.

A New Side of Life.

ANET has once more left her home, never again to return and remain there, except for only a day now and again. She is now in Innerleithen, in charge of the children of a family in good position there. Her duties are light and pleasant; she walks with her little charge along the banks of the Tweed and the Leithen, and round the Pirn Hill; she drinks in the beauty of the lovely scenery, and meets with young companions. The sadness that often clouded her brow when she sat on "the greystone" at the side of St Mary's Loch has disappeared, and she is cheerful and gay. Yet a new trial meets her here. There is no family worship, and there might as well be no God for all she could learn in this house. On the contrary, it was quite a common thing to have parties on Saturday nights, and these often encroached on the Sabbath morning. On one of these occasions they had a dance, and when the clock was on the stroke of twelve, the master of the house stepped into the lobby and turned the hands back to ten, and the giddy dance went on. Janet observed this, and was shocked and terror-stricken. The kitchen floor was laid with flagstones, and one of them was cracked in the centre. While Janet is thinking of the daring act of her master, and listening to the dancing and mirth on this Sabbath morning, her eye gets fixed on the broken flagstone, and she imagines that she sees it moving. Is God opening the floor that the earth may swallow them up for their wickedness? She trembles from head to foot, and falls on her knees and cries out, "Lord, be merciful to us sinners." Her fellow-servant, who appeared to have no fear of God, not only laughs at her, but tells her companions, who in turn laugh and make a mock of what they call "Janet's earthquake." Janet herself feels ashamed—or, rather, acts as if she were—and joins in the laugh; but her conscience is ill at ease; and when she retires to bed and begins to repeat her hymns, part of that blessed one, which she had learned from her mother's lips, comes forcibly to her memory—

> Ashamed of Jesus! yes I may,
> When I've no guilt to wash away;
> No tear to wipe, no good to crave,
> No fear to quell, no soul to save.

Like Peter, she weeps bitterly, and vows never again to be ashamed of Jesus; but she has yet to learn how weak she is, and that it is from God alone she must draw strength to serve Him. She goes on making vows and breaking them. Then her companions are all gay and merry; she is young, may she not also have a little fun? She, like the 'Young

Cottager,' will turn very good when she comes to die. She has a garret room where she can say her prayers unobserved; and she will take her mother's advice and say them always before she is too wearied. But when she runs up to her room for this purpose, she is always in such a hurry to get down to the kitchen again, that she may join in the sport of her fellow-servant and young friends; and sometimes as she goes through the form of praying she scarcely knows what she is saying. Poor Janet! she is " sowing to the wind," and " will reap the whirlwind."

We pass over much that might be interesting to her nieces, but too tedious to relate. Let it suffice for the present to say that Janet has been two years here, but whatever she has gained in strength and worldly station, she has lost in piety. She has, however, given satisfaction to her mistress, who is very unwilling to part with her.

After some round-about roads we meet her again, somewhat in her right mind, in the service of Mrs Smith, the widow of an English clergyman. She has one daughter, and keeps a lady boarder. Miss Smith reads prayers every morning, and the Sabbath is observed with due reverence. Janet gets to church " Sunday about " with her fellow-servant. Mrs Smith gives her some good books to read. Her fellow-servant is well-inclined, and they take sweet counsel together. Oh, how much happier she is now! She had been drinking of the world's polluted waters, and found they could not quench her thirst. She has sinned. She will do so no more; she will henceforth slake her thirst at the fountain of for-giving love.   Prayer is again a pleasure, and her Bible a delight.

Although the family is small, they keep a great deal of company.   White dresses were greatly worn by young ladies in those days, and the washing of these was a heavy part of the servants' work.   Janet has this to do, and, being yet in her teens, she is often so wearied that at night she is hardly able to read a few verses in her Bible.   But she hears the Scriptures read in the morning; she is kindly treated, and is contented and happy.   Like Job, she had twice lost all her earthly possessions; true, they were not thousands of sheep, oxen, and camels, but, however little, they were her all; yet no murmur es-caped her lips, and she did not charge God foolishly. Hitherto she had enjoyed good health; now that God is about to touch her bone and flesh, will she curse Him to His face?   We shall see.   We have hinted that Janet's work was too heavy for one of her age.   Mrs Smith's was a large house, with many apartments, and the greater part fell to Janet to keep in order.

It is the month of June, during Janet's second half-year in this place; and one morning she is lying in a room at the top of the large house, un-able to lift her head from the pillow.   The doctor is sent for; he pronounces her in a high fever, and bleeds her.   The family are in perplexity.   Mrs Langhorn (a married daughter of Mrs Smith) has come to be in her mother's house during her con-finement.   The other servant has her hands full;

and Janet's mother is sent for to come and take her home. But, alas! sister Bella is lying dangerously ill there, so that her mother cannot leave. An elder sister, who has been some time married, has one of her children dying of whooping cough, and she cannot get to Janet's assistance. She lies in this garret room for five weeks ere she can lift her head, and it is other two weeks before she can go downstairs. Bleeding was at that time much practised by doctors, and during her illness she has been three times bled; and her suffering and weakness are extreme. Her only attendant is her fellow-servant — poor overwrought Ann. She looks into the room every morning, and fills the jug with water (for Janet's thirst is great). She visits her again in the evening, and performs the same duty, sits by her a few minutes and weeps, for she thinks her friend is dying.

But what are Janet's thoughts in this time of suffering and solitude? She has many reproaches for herself as she thinks of her light-hearted folly at Innerleithen. Surely her sins have found her out, God has set them before her eyes. She believes she is dying, and where are all her resolutions to prepare for death? She cannot read, she cannot pray; must she perish for ever? The anguish of her soul overbalances her bodily suffering. She thinks on her father's remarks about Dr Lawson's prayers at her baptism. She is sure that her mother and father will be praying for her, and she knows that the fervent prayer of the righteous availeth much. If she gets better she will live a different life, she will not leave the preparation for death till she lies on a

I

sick-bed. Poor Janet! she has yet to learn that she cannot buy eternal life by her prayers or reformation—that eternal life is the gift of God, who giveth liberally and does not cast up sin; yet does He say, "Seek, and ye shall find; knock, and it shall be opened unto you." So far as her knowledge goes, she is seeking, and is therefore in the way of finding.

Let not her nieces think this story of Janet's suffering, mentally as well as bodily, overdrawn. Nay, it is solemn truth, and the half has not been told. But they may learn from what has been said to seek God while He is near, to call on Him while He hears, lest when their fear cometh the Wisdom they would not heed shall laugh at their calamity.

The last of the seven weeks that Janet spent in her lonely room she is able to get out of bed for the greater part of each day, and she moves about in order to try her strength. She insists on Ann bringing up to her the knives, forks, and spoons, and these she manages to clean for her. She is grieved to see her burdened on her account, and so wearied out at night; but at least they are now able to pray together, as their wont was before Janet's illness, and to comfort one another. Janet now thinks she will be able to go downstairs, but when she makes the attempt the joints of her knees are so loosened and weak that she cannot balance herself. The only way in which she can accomplish her purpose is to turn round and creep backwards down the two long flights of stairs, and this she does for many a day.

She is kindly and considerately treated, and she gathers strength, though very slowly; is it to be wondered at, having been so weakened by the draining away of her life's blood, and so nigh unto death ?

It is now autumn. Janet is yet far from her former strength, and she fears the winter, and the heavier work which it will bring. Soon there will be the parties, with the late hours and early rising ; she thinks of giving up her situation, and throws out a hint of her intention. But Mrs Smith will not hear of such a thing, and says it will be very ungrateful on her part to leave after she has lived so long in the house doing nothing, and that she must reconsider her decision and remain. Janet is grieved, for she does not wish to be ungrateful; but she fears that she will not be able to do the work expected of her. She weeps, but she also prays to God to forgive the past, and that He will guide her in the future. Her prayers now are not a formal repeating of words, but with her whole heart she cries, " Lord, be merciful to me, a sinner." In all this sore trouble Janet sins not with her mouth, nor charges God foolishly. And He has not forgotten to be gracious; for, behold, deliverance is near.

XVIII.

In a New Sphere.

ABOUT this time the letter-carrier, one morning, hands Janet, among other letters, one addressed to herself. She does not know the handwriting, and is not a little puzzled with the contents, which are as follows :—

"31 Howe Street, Edinburgh.

"Mrs Robert Scott-Moncrieff wishes very much to see Janet Greenfield at above address as soon as possible for her to come."

Janet had never heard the name before. Who can the writer be? What can she want? she asks herself. Ann advises her to go, and suggests that perhaps the lady has heard something about her purpose of leaving her present situation, and may wish to engage her. Janet asks and obtains leave from Mrs Smith, and early next morning sets out for Edinburgh to get the mystery solved.

After some difficulty she finds the street and number, rings the door bell, and is ushered into a fine drawing-room. To her surprise, who should welcome her but her old friend Miss Susan Pringle, now Mrs

Scott-Moncrieff? She had been married for some years, and had three little girls. She had been wishing much to have Janet as one of her servants, but had lost trace of her; and it was only the other day, she said, that she learned through one of her father-in-law's servants where Janet was. So the mystery is solved; and Janet is seated by her old friend, who has many kindly inquiries to make regarding her since they parted at Yair.

She also inquires about the work she has been accustomed to, and learns of her illness; and soon saw that in her present state of weakness she was utterly unfit to undertake another winter's such work. Janet has no ill to say of any one but herself, she does not speak of unkind treatment; and Mrs Scott-Moncrieff is pleased to see that that feature of her character, which she had discerned in her childhood, had not been blurred by the tear and wear of the world. Then she said, " Janet, I have a situation vacant, that of under-nurserymaid, and I will be pleased if you will accept it. Your wages will not be so much as where you are, but your work will be lighter; and if I find that your behaviour is good, you will have the first opening among the higher servants."

Janet expresses her thanks, and says, " Ma'am, for the love I bear you, I could serve you for nothing." She gets her arles, and returns to Musselburgh with a glad heart. The green map comes strongly to her remembrance, and she is sure that it has a great deal to do with her good fortune that day. On reaching home, she acquaints Mrs Smith with her engagement, and begs of her not to think her ungrateful; for she would not have left her service but from a dread of not being able to do the work, and of again being laid up by illness. And, lest she should misunderstand her motive, she tells her she is getting less wages, but lighter work. Mrs Smith sees that Janet has been only slowly gathering strength, she sees also the force of her argument, and says she is satisfied with her reasons for taking another situation; but, as she had pleased her well, she very much regrets her leaving.

It is a comfort to Janet to know that she retains the goodwill of the family, and for the few remaining weeks she does everything for their comfort; and when she leaves she gets a present from each member of the household, and is asked to visit them when she can. Janet has tried to follow her mother's advice to do everything in her power to live peaceably with those she served, and to always leave a welcome behind her.

On the appointed day she arrives at 31 Howe Street, accompanied by a porter carrying her little trunk. She goes to the kitchen, where the servants give her a kindly welcome, but throw out some unpleasant hints about the head nurserymaid, to the effect that if she should make out a half-year under her it is more than any one has done before. Then they show her upstairs to the nursery, and say that after the children are in bed she is to come down, and some of them will give her a lift up with the trunk. Janet gets rather a dry welcome from her superior, Jenny Forsyth, but she is delighted with the little girls, who draw around her and tell her that Mamma says she is to be their maid, and is to be called "Jessie," to make a distinction between her and Jenny Forsyth. Janet is set to work, the children get supper, and are put to bed; and when all is put to rights, Janet respectfully asks leave to go downstairs for her trunk. Granting this, Jenny charges her not to put off her time gossiping with the servants, as that is a thing she will not allow. On getting downstairs she asks the housemaid to help her up with her trunk, but the cook says, "What's all your hurry? You will have been getting some new dresses; you must be neighbourly, and let us see them."

Janet in her simplicity hastens to open her trunk, shows a new dress, and is about to shut her trunk, when they laugh, and remark to each other that she is not up to the custom. The cook says, "Jessie— I suppose that is to be your name; weel, Jessie, have you not brought a bottle with you, to give your new fellow-servants a dram? I can tell 'e that unless you creesh their feet you'll have something to do to make your way among them."

"I never," says Janet, "heard of such a thing, nor thought of such a thing."

"Oh, maybe not," says the laundrymaid, "but it's not too late to learn. Give me a half-crown, and I will run out for a bottle."

"I never bought whisky," says Jessie, "nor will I, for I don't think it is right."

Then they laugh again, and the cook says, "Maybe she has spent all her siller on her new dress, to take the shine off us. Here, I'll lend you a shilling, no to see you beat."

But no, no; Jessie will not yield. Sarah, the housemaid, feels for her, and says, " Come away, Jessie, I'll give you a lift with your trunk ; maybe, you'll treat us all when you get your ' Christmas ' from the children."

Sarah charges her to say nothing about the whisky to Jenny, or she will run to the mistress with it ; and they will all get their leave. Jenny scolds Jessie for putting off her time downstairs, and says, " The cook will have been stuffing you like a dead turkey, as she has done to all them before you—no to their profit."

Poor Jessie is perplexed, and feels that her position is likely to be a difficult one. Her work may be lighter, but her trouble, she fears, will be greater. She weeps and prays. Oh, that she could but see her mother, to tell her her sorrows and get her advice !

Her mistress sends for Janet to come and speak with her in her bedroom. She says she is glad to see her looking a little stronger, and gives her many good counsels on her duties and her privileges. Then she asks her to read a chapter, and is glad to hear her read so well ; she gives her the ' Pilgrim's Progress,' so that she can read a little to Jenny every night after her work is done. She prays with her, and then sends her away, bidding her tell Jenny that she wishes to see her.

What passed between Jenny and the mistress was not known, but when Janet showed her the book, and told her that she was to read it to her,

Jenny says, " Oh, yes. So I am to be instructed by her favourite."

Jenny had been four years in the family, and was considered a trustworthy servant; but she had a very bad temper, was jealous of her honour, and suspicious of any one standing higher in her mistress's favour than herself. She had no liking to hear the praises of Janet sounded by Mrs Pringle, and many attempts she made to lessen her in the estimation of the household, but when the accusations were looked into they always turned out in Janet's favour.

A few weeks passed away. The little girls become passionately fond of their young nurse, and she is daily gaining favour downstairs. Even Jenny has grown somewhat kindly. About this time, a little girl of seven years, a granddaughter of Mrs Pringle, is on her way home from India, in order to complete her education. Mrs Pringle is making preparations for her reception, and has come to Howe Street to consult with her daughter, Mrs Scott-Moncrieff; and they arrange that Janet and the two eldest girls are to go to Yair, to be there to meet their cousin, Mary Pringle, and that they shall remain as companions for her. Janet is to be maid to the three, for at least a few months.

Oh, what a memorable day for Janet when the Yair carriage comes to the door to carry Grandmamma and her two little granddaughters to Yair. Janet runs downstairs to bid her fellow-servants good-bye; they clap her, kiss her, and bid her Godspeed, saying there is little chance for Haman when Mordecai is on the king's horse. Jenny also, with some good grace, bids her good-bye, hoping that those who are honouring her now will not be disappointed "when they know her better."

As the carriage approached Yair house, Janet could not help thinking of the contrast with that day when she went to explain her green map, and she gives God the thanks of her heart for all the goodness He had made to pass before her. She is congratulated by the butler and by some of the female servants who had known her as a little lassie in the days when she used to get her lessons in sewing. She is taken up to the third floor of the lovely mansion and shown into the north room, a large and commodious apartment having a small room opening from it, in which a window to the front takes in the view of the silvery Tweed and Fernielea. There are also two windows at the end, under which a little brook goes rippling past, with flowers and trees on the bank beyond. Janet is lost in admiration and wonder; she is almost persuaded that the whole is a dream.

In a few days the little girl from India arrives, accompanied by a black woman servant. What a contrast there is between the two! Miss Mary Pringle has very lovely pale blue eyes, and a profusion of flaxen hair flows over her shoulders. She is attired in a green silk pelisse and white frock. Her ayah is dressed in a purple skirt and white, loose spencer; she is bare-headed, and her long black hair is plaited, coiled up, and fastened by a silver comb. She wears silver earrings, in the shape of little bells, a string of yellow beads round her neck, and two or three silver rings on her fingers.

Everything was done that could be thought of to make Miss Mary's arrival a happy one, but she rejects all caresses, and clings to her black maid, like a loving child to a tender mother. She can speak English, and Hindustani as well. In this language she converses with her ayah, and sometimes weeps bitterly, but not a word of English will she speak to any of her friends. The couple are shown into the bow room next to Janet's, in order to familiarise them in time with each other, but Mary repels all her approaches to kindness. The Indian woman and Janet, however, very soon get warm friends. The former can speak English well, and she tells Janet that Mary is one of the most loving and love-able of children, but she knows that she (her attendant) is to return to India in a few days, and she wishes to go back with her to her own happy home. Janet herself weeps, for her early experience enables her to understand Mary's bitter sorrow. The ayah tells Mary that Janet had been sent away from her own home when she was a child, and that she feels for Mary and loves her. Mary, hearing this gives a kind look to Janet, but keeps close to the other, with her arms round her neck, hugging and kissing her— all of which is a great mystery to her little cousins.

The day appointed for the ayah's return to India has arrived. Mrs Pringle and Janet enter the bow room, and grandmamma tells Mary that she now must bid her maid farewell, for Janet is henceforward to be her attendant. The parting is heart-rending. Janet had thought that the children of the rich had no trials, but she sees differently now. Grandmamma locks the room door, takes her seat by the window, and commences her knitting; and Mary, in the anguish of her soul, throws herself upon the floor, crying, "Oh papa, mamma, oh ayah, dear ayah, come back and take me to my happy home—cruel grandmamma! I will die; yes, I will die."

All Janet's attempts to soothe Mary's grief are unavailing, and she lies down beside her and weeps in silence. Bed-time comes, and Mary's crib is removed to Janet's room. The little one is undressed and put to bed, but she continues to cry bitterly, and becomes fevered and restless. Janet falls on her knees and prays for her; then, sick at heart, she sits by the bedside till morning, dreading the awakening, which will only renew her sorrow. Mary looks up and says, "Jessie, have you not been to bed?"

"No, darling, you were ill, and I could not leave you."

Mary raised herself up, threw her arms around Janet's neck, saying, "Kind, loving Jessie, you will be my ayah now."

So the two hearts were then united till death brake the bond. True friendship halves sorrows and shares joys, whether they come to rich or to poor.

All now goes on well; a governess is engaged, and the three cousins commence their education together. Janet's duties are light, and consist only of her attendance on the three misses. She often takes her seam and sits in the schoolroom while they are at their lessons, paying close attention to the pronouncing of words, and going over the spelling after them ; and thus she is, unobserved, gathering more learning and knowledge for herself. Miss Ronald, the governess, is an amiable young lady, and Janet and she, being much together, are soon close friends.

Six months have been passed at Yair. Mrs Scott-Moncrieff now requires to have Janet with her, and she calls her and the two children home ; and now when Mary is left alone with her governess, she becomes again uncontrollable. She refuses her food, will not say her lessons, and cries night and day when awake for her much loved maid, "Jessie." At last, arrangements are made for Mary to go to Edinburgh for the winter. A tutor is engaged to come in for some hours every day to give her and her cousins lessons—an arrangement which gave Mary great joy, for she and her cousins and "Jessie" will be together again. Janet understood that she had given much satisfaction at Yair, and now that Mary is again under her care, Jenny Forsyth is told that "Jessie" is not to be any longer under her, but on an equal footing with her, and that she is to have the sole care of the three misses of the family, along with Miss Mary Pringle. Jenny feels somewhat indignant at the thought of being put on a level with a girl in her teens, and resigns her situation. It was thought that she was a little disappointed when it was readily accepted, and not a little mortified to see "Jessie" promoted to her place.

At the following November term Janet becomes head nurserymaid in charge of all the children, Mary Pringle included, and a girl about Janet's own age is engaged as under nurserymaid. She is named Grace Dickson, a quiet, warm-hearted young woman. Janet put on no airs in her new position; the thought of looking down on any one below her was far from her mind. She and Grace work to each other's hands. They also are one in setting the Lord always before them, so they are united in heart and hand; and during the sixty years and more which went over their heads after that, with all their various changes, there was not a single break in their friendship.

When the children are all put to bed, Janet and Grace read the 'Pilgrim's Progress' and the 'Annals of the Poor;' the one sewing and the other reading, alternately. They are happy, and they seek no other society; the children are joyful, and the servants below are obliging and kind. Mrs Scott-Moncrieff is pleased and satisfied with her new arrangements. Janet has never felt so happy as now since she left her own early home; " peace and plenty " is the order of the house, and so the winter months pass pleasantly away.

In February it is thought advisable to send Mary Pringle to a boarding-school, and shortly after this a baby boy is born to the family. Mrs Scott-Moncrieff recovers but slowly; the baby is a little, feeble thing, and it is thought necessary to get in a wet nurse. A kindly, healthy woman is got; and so, by Mary's leaving and this arrangement, Janet's cares and troubles are greatly lightened.

XIX.

An Entanglement.

THE housemaid, Sarah, and Janet had been very friendly with each other ever since she helped her up the stairs with her trunk. A young man belonging to Queensferry had been paying his addresses to Sarah, and Janet was let into the secret. She had been introduced to him, James Henderson by name, a respectable tradesman, and he has a companion named William Sharp. Sarah suggests that James should bring Willie in; how nice it would be for Janet to have a sweetheart also. Then it is proposed that on a set day James will bring Willie; Sarah and Janet will ask leave for the afternoon; and they will have a walk. Janet agrees, the day appointed comes round, and Sarah and she get leave of absence for the afternoon. The two young men arrive, and Janet is introduced to Willie. He has a frank, kindly manner; is tall, good-looking, and dressed (according to the fashion of the time) in white linen tweeled trousers, yellow vest, light blue coat, with a yellow

silk handkerchief hanging half out of the pocket.
He wore a white hat, which latter article recalls to
Janet's memory a remark of her father's, when one
told him that he had seen his eldest son, quite a
gentleman, with a white hat—" When I see a man
with a white hat, I always conclude that there is a
fool beneath it."

Janet, unobserved, smiles at James's and Sarah's
idea of a sweetheart. Do they think she will draw
up with a fop? In the meantime it will be nice to
have a walk, but she forgets that it is written, " Go
not in the way of the wicked, lest ye learn their
ways ; and they that trust in their own strength are
fools." But whatever Janet thinks of Willie, he is
captivated with her; and he tells James that, by hook
or by crook, he will have her for a wife. Sarah in
due course communicates this to Janet, who laughs
at the idea ; and she lets Sarah understand that she
will not consent to receive further visits from Willie.
Meanwhile, Sarah's marriage day is fixed ; Willie
loads her with presents, and begs her to favour him
by making Janet her best maid, as he is to be best
man. Sarah agrees, and Janet, unaware of the plot,
consents. Moreover, Willie sends her a string of
beads for the occasion, and she is much pleased with
Sarah's respect and confidence. As Janet has never
asked a holiday since she entered Mrs Scott-Moncrieff's service, she readily grants her three days ; so
that she may not only be at the marriage, but accompany Sarah to her new home, and go to church with
her on the Sabbath. Janet and Sarah are delighted,
Willie and James are overjoyed ; and they think

there may yet be a match between Willie and Janet. On the marriage day, Janet is dressed in a white frock, with white sash around her waist; and she has the beads about her neck. Grace, who was endowed with considerable shrewdness, and not above employing the art of flattery at times, declares that she is like an angel, and is sure to throw dust in the shoemaker's eye; but she must take care that she does not blind her own—a very needful hint at this stage of Janet's history.

The marriage comes off to the satisfaction of all concerned. Willie pays all possible attention to Janet, and asks her to take a walk with him on the Sabbath afternoon, to which she consents. He introduces her to his relatives, accompanies her home on the Monday, and insists on her promising to receive a weekly visit from him. This she cannot do, but she promises to write, and let him know when it will be convenient to see him.

On her return home Janet is pleased with everything and everybody, but when she gets to her little room and thinks over all that has passed in the three days—though pleased with everything else, she is greatly displeased with herself: conscience had not been silent, but she had turned a deaf ear; and now, alone, and conscious that God's eye is looking upon her heart, she is ashamed. She cannot pray; she has not only kept company with a man who thought it no shame to take God's holy name in vain, but she found that she loved him, and had also broken God's holy day. Oh, what a net she had spread for her feet by promising to write to him! How shall the snare be broken? If she should promise to marry him, she will make him promise to turn over a new leaf. But then the Scripture says, "Be not unequally yoked with unbelievers," and she could not expect God to bless a union that He had forbidden. Oh, if she could pray and confess her sins! But would God hear her prayers while she loved one at enmity with Him? A double mind is an abomination to Him. In her anguish she cries, " Lord, help me, lest I perish!"

Janet remembers that when her mother was in trouble she used to take down the Bible and lift up her heart to God, and ask, that by pointing her finger on a text, that text might guide her in a right way. Afterwards she did not think this a right way of coming to know God's will, but at this stage of Janet's history she did not see it to be wrong. So she takes down her Bible, lifts up her heart to God, begging Him to give her a sure token of the way wherein she should walk, so that she might follow in the way He pointed out. She closes her eyes, opens her Bible, puts her finger on it, opens her eyes and reads these words, " If thou wilt walk in the ways of thy father David, I will build thee a house." She feels that God had spoken to her. It was none of the ways of David to keep company with wicked and ungodly men: he had not gone in with dissemblers, and he prayed that God would not gather His soul with sinners.

Janet might have known all this before. She knows it now, however; she falls on her knees and gives thanks to God and asks strength from

Him, and vows that henceforth she will never keep company with any man that takes strong drink, swears, or strolls about on the Sabbath. Whatever God means by building her a house, she knows He will keep his word; and she will trust Him. So she rises from her knees, hurriedly gets pen and paper, lest her resolution should fail her, and she writes to Willie, stating that, seeing he is a man that does not fear God, she cannot henceforth have anything more to do with him. She adds that she will receive no more visits from him, and her letter does not require an answer. Willie makes further attempts to see her, but Janet keeps firm to her vows.

The family had a country house in the neighbourhood of South Queensferry, where they used to spend the summer months. Janet looks forward to the summer with trembling, lest she should there come in contact with Willie (who lives in the neighbourhood), and fall before a new temptation. But God can make a way of escape, and He will not suffer her to be tempted above what she is able to bear. As in former days, so now deliverance comes from a very unexpected quarter. Mr Scott-Moncrieff is at this time appointed chamberlain to the Duke of Buccleuch, and the family remove to Dalkeith, instead of going, as they would otherwise have done, to Queensferry. Here in the beautiful grounds of Dalkeith House, Janet walks with her young charge amongst the flowers, or sits under the shade of the chestnut trees, now in blossom; and as she inhales the sweet fragrance and enjoys the beautiful scenery, she sings Cowper's hymn—

The calm retreat, the silent shade,
  With praise and prayer agree,
And seem by Thy sweet bounty made
  For those that follow Thee;

Then if the spirit meet the soul,
  And grace her pure abode,
With what sweet peace and love and joy
  She communes with her God;

There like the nightingale she pours
  Her solitary lays,
Nor asks a witness of her song,
  Nor thirsts for human praise.

XX.

Love Makes Labour Light.

ABOUT this time Janet is called to her first deep sorrow, the death of her beloved sister Bella, who had long been a great sufferer, in body and in soul. When she was awakened to a sense of her spiritual needs, God had used Janet as a channel through which she drank of the water of life, and the love of each for the other was very great. Janet felt desolate and almost inconsolable, but at this time her piety was greatly deepened. Much of her spare time was spent in reading good books, and committing to memory psalms and hymns and portions of the Bible. All attempts of her fellow-servants to draw her into their worldly amusements were unavailing. Many an effort was made to get her to join them in their folly, but she had already suffered too deeply to yield again. She keeps her vows and sings—

> As I, glad, bid adieu to the world's fancied pleasure,
> You pity my weakness. Alas! did you know
> The joys of religion, that vast hidden treasure;
> Could you have me forsake them?
>   Oh, never! Oh, no!

But in those brighter paths that you call melancholy,
  I've found the delights the world cannot know;
I know by experience in whom I've believed;
  Would you have me forsake Him?
                    Oh, never! Oh, no!

A new circumstance, arising from the delicate
health of the little boy that was born into the
family before they left Edinburgh, now intervenes.
This child, on being weaned, is given over to the
care of Janet. His condition is such that it is
thought necessary to send him to Edinburgh, in
order that he may be under higher medical skill.
Another servant is engaged to assist in the nursery,
whilst Janet and her suffering charge go to live with
the sick boy's widowed grandmother—Mrs Pringle,
lately of Yair—in Charlotte Square.

Here, at the top of the large house, in a neat, comfortable room, we find Janet and the sick child, lonely
enough; for though the servants in the family are all
very respectful, there is not one of them who sym-
pathises with her religious cast of mind. For many
weeks the little sufferer and his nurse are left very
much to themselves, and yet they are not alone.
Janet has her Bible, other good books, and her God,
to whom she tells all her sorrow, and with these she
has companions enough.

Among other modes of treatment for the suffering
child, vapour baths are recommended. To secure
these, Janet with her charge is carried daily in a
Sedan chair to the head of Leith Walk, and she is
required to sit for a quarter of an hour in a vapour
bath, with her boy on her knee. She always dressed

him before putting on her own clothes, and thus she caught a chest cold which induced shortness of breathing, and troubled her less or more throughout her life. The treatment, however, proves unavailing for the poor sufferer. After this Janet is sent to the sea-side, and here and there, for change of air; sometimes along with the other children, but generally accompanied only by the sick boy; and this goes on for years.

The nature of the child's suffering made him very restless through the night, and his nurse walks up and down the room for hours, hushing her darling boy to rest in her arms. But her long nursing, with its toil and anxiety, tells upon her own health in the shape of loss of appetite and physical exhaustion, and the bloom again fades from her cheek. Her mother and other friends, when they learn all the truth, get somewhat alarmed; and the former comes to Dalkeith to persuade her to give up her charge and go home for a little rest. But Janet answers all their counsels and entreaties by saying that the nature of the child's trouble made it difficult for a stranger to do her duty. "God has called me to this work," she said, "and I will not give it up; I will nurse my darling boy while he requires it. If he dies, I will die with him. And, dear mother, you know that love makes labour light."

She continues her nursing, and does not cease to pray earnestly in the poor child's behalf; and after three weary years she sees with joy that his health begins to improve. "Jessie's" presence had become indispensable to him, and this made her in a great measure a prisoner ; but she is now allowed an hour in one day of the week to take a walk or see a friend.   Her brother Willie, who had served his apprenticeship as a saddler, is now working as a journeyman in Dalkeith, and it is a great delight for Janet to meet her brother in the evening and have a walk in the Duke's parks.   By this means and her walks during the day with her precious charge, she regains her health and cheerfulness in some measure.   She has now been more than six years in the service of the family ; four of which had been occupied in nursing, as she has described.

XXI.

Marriage.

AT length an event takes place which makes a complete change of circumstances. The date is the 20th of January, 1832. On that day the children are in high spirits, and there are to be no lessons. The drawing-room is decorated with flowers. The little misses are dressed in white, the boys are in their Sunday jackets, each with a bow of white ribbon on his breast. It is Janet's wedding day; she is to be married in the drawing-room; and Miss Eliza is to be bridesmaid. The servants are hurrying through their work, for there is to be a grand supper in the hall. The young ladies are arraying Janet in white; and her head-dress is of their mamma's making. Dear little Robert (the one she has tended so long) has looked a little suspicious all the day, and never loses sight of Janet for a moment; and when he sees her dressed, he says, "My Jessie is a lady." But when he is told that she is going away, no more to return, his outburst of grief is heart-rending to witness, and Janet's breast heaves with emotion.

But why have we up to the present said nothing about the bridegroom ? Just because the record of Janet's history is not intended to be a love story, but to show the wonderful leading of God's providence, and that others may be helped to put their trust in Him—to show that He is unchangeable, and brings about His purposes now, as in the days of old, by ordinary means, and yet by leading the blind by a way that they know not.

We will now, however, give a short outline of the early life of Janet's intended husband, which will enable us to see if she has kept her vows. James Kemp was born in humble circumstances; his father was a shepherd, a quiet, industrious, God-fearing man ; his mother, a very godly woman, was converted in early life under the preaching of White-field. James, their first-born, was apprenticed to a saddler in East Linton, Haddingtonshire. He was of a lively temperament, attentive to his work, and anxious to excel in it ; he could not do anything by halves, but what he did he strove to have it perfect. This was the rule he laid down for himself, but he did not always manage to keep by it. After shop hours he joined companions in sports and games, and was so fond of amusement that it often occupied his thoughts so much while at work as to cause him to make blunders. These were always a grief to him, and he would weep over them in the night, and say to himself, "If I continue to play with these bowls, I shall never learn any trade." He prays to God to help him to deny himself in this matter, and then rises and runs to a bridge, over which he throws his bowl bag and its contents into the water. "There you go," said he, "you shall not make a botch of me, I shall be master of my trade." And here is seen the future man in the boy.

He had an old maiden aunt living in the village. She, like his mother, was a convert of Whitefield's, and a pious woman. In the winter nights, after shop hours, she coaxes James to read to her, and takes care that the books she puts into his hands are good and profitable. He thus gets a taste for reading, and this, coupled with the religious training at home, results in his mother's counsels to him becoming more deeply impressed on his mind. In course of time he finishes his apprenticeship; gets a certificate from his master, which he thinks overdrawn; for he is too honest to drink in flattery, and hates shams. Then he sets off to London, in order to get further insight into his trade. After a time he comes north to Wooler, where he is engaged as foreman in the shop of a Mr Morton, in whose employment he remains for four years. Here he is much pained to see the desecration of the Sabbath; the youths after the forenoon service betaking themselves to amusements as on ordinary days. His thirst for reading had not diminished, but his stock of books is small. On the Saturday evenings he would go to a secondhand book-stall, select a book, sometimes so worn that it will scarcely hold together; but he manages to bind it, and in course of time he has got together a somewhat decent library. On Sabbath afternoons, when the weather is favourable, he seeks retirement on the hill-side.

These he finds seasons of pure enjoyment, and he there stores his mind with knowledge, and worships his God.

In his lodgings there is no recognition of God in any way, and, though otherwise comfortable, he fears the coming of the winter nights, when he would have no facilities for calm reading and thought. But God is planning for him in this matter. As he sits alone in his room, he hears the voice of a female singing, always at a set hour. He listens, and concludes that the person is engaged in God's worship. He remarks that she gives out the line of the evening hymn, and yet he hears only one voice. Naturally, his curiosity is excited, and he makes some inquiry of his land-lady about her next door neighbour. He learns that she is a widow, an old Scotchwoman; and James makes up his mind to call on her, and claim friend-ship with her as a countryman. Next evening he raps at the door and says, " May a Scotchman come in?" " You may," replied the inmate, "if you are the true blue, and believe in the Covenants."

" Well, good woman," said James, " I believe in God; and I lodge at the other end of the wall. I thought I heard you worshipping after the way of our Scotch fathers, and I am come in to get a crack with you. When we were—that is my brothers and sisters—too young to read, my father at family wor-ship gave out the line, so that we might all join in the singing of the Psalm, but I noticed that you gave out the line though you are alone, and wondered that you stopped to do so, and did not just go on singing."

" Eh, man, ye suirely ha'e little brains. Do ye no

see that the oftener I read the precious word, it grows the sweeter to my taste—aye, sweeter than honey to my mouth."

Thus there is the beginning of a friendship that continued as long as the old woman lived; James keeping up the correspondence in the shape of a present of tea and sugar at Christmas time. He soon becomes a lodger with the old Scotchwoman; she hails him as a son, and he looks on her as a mother. The minister whom James sat under at Wooler was also a Scotchman—an aged, infirm, old bachelor; and with this old man he spent many a winter's evening. While he soothed him by many kind acts, the old man helped him greatly in the ways of righteousness, and supplied him with reading of a helpful kind.

This continued for the four years James was in the town, and on leaving, he and a young man of the same trade had made up their minds to go out to America. It was a sore trial to the aged minister to part with James, who by his happy disposition and kindly ways had cheered many hours for the old man, which would have been times of loneliness to him; and he in turn had reaped a harvest of knowledge which it would have been difficult for him to have acquired otherwise.

On the day that James went to bid his dear old friend farewell, among other good counsels the old man gave him was this—

"James," he said, "I would counsel you, when young, to look out for a godly woman and marry her. You see how old and frail I am—what would

I give now for a gentle, warm-hearted Christian wife? God once brought me in contact with such an one, but I was in no hurry to marry, and I let her slip. Don't you follow my example in this. A wiser man than I am—Luther, the great reformer—said the sweetest thing in this world is a pious woman's heart."

"Your counsel, sir," said James, "I believe is good; but where am I to find such a woman? I have not as yet met with one."

"Listen to me, James. You may not know where to find her, but put the case into God's hands, trust Him; and though she be at the ends of the earth, He can bring her to you."

"Thank you, sir, for your advice and encouragement. I had a God-fearing mother, for whom I have worn mourning for five years, and in heart I will mourn for her while I live. If God should be pleased to bring me in contact with such an one as she was, I would marry her to-morrow."

The two friends part, not again to meet here below. James sets off for Edinburgh, where, according to appointment, he expects to meet his companion. There they are to make all arrangements for sailing to America. The day, the hour appointed for meeting comes, and James is there; but there is no appearance of his friend. He waits for several days, but the friend fails to keep his appointment. While waiting on, he observes an advertisement in a newspaper that a journeyman saddler is wanted at Dalkeith. As the distance is only six miles, he thinks he might go out, more for the sake of putting off the time than to apply for the situation. Indeed he had no intention of entering into any new engagement. Leaving a note at the inn where he was staying, in case his friend should call in his absence, he starts for Dalkeith. He calls on Mr ———, who had been advertising for a man, and he proposes to engage him at once. He offers him good wages to begin with, and holds out the prospect of a rise. The foreman of the establishment is an old man, who is getting very deaf, and is likely to resign soon, and James will probably succeed him. The inducements to accept the situation are tempting, but he will not engage at once; he will think over the matter, and give an answer in a few days. Still in the hope that his friend will cast up, he waits on, but there is no appearance of him, and no explanation from him. James then returns to Dalkeith, completes the engagement, and enters on his new situation. And this, it may be mentioned, was only three days before Janet comes with Mr Scott-Moncrieff's family to live in the town.

James one day was taunted and teased a little by his brother for taking a roundabout road to America and landing at Dalkeith. He did not enter into any disputation with him on the subject, but he meekly answered, "Is there not a cause? It is not in man that walketh to direct his own steps; every little step I take the gloom flies from the past; and though the way is dark to me at times I am not perplexed. It is all light to God."

XXII.

Love at First Sight.

THE Duke's Chamberlain in those days was always elected to the office of Bailie, and Mr Scott-Moncrieff is henceforth known by the name of the "new Bailie." A few days after the family arrive in Dalkeith, Janet and two of the children are sent out to make some purchases; and among other things sponges are required for the nursery. For these articles she is directed to Mr Simpson's (the saddler's), and his new assistant attends to the customer. Their eyes meet, and a thrilling emotion passes through their hearts. In that glance James has seen his future wife, and Janet her future husband. But both are ignorant of the fact; and, strange as it may appear, three long years pass before they meet again.

After Janet leaves the shop, James remarks to his fellow-workmen, "What a comely young woman that is, and so pleasant a manner she has." They reply that she is one of the new Bailie's servants, and they laughingly advise him not to lose sight of her for a wife, saying that if she is a favourite with the Bailie he may get an introduction to his grace the Duke of Buccleuch—at which they all take a hearty laugh. James replies, " I understand the greater part of the tradesmen in Dalkeith worship the Duke's golden calf, but I have no intention of becoming an idol worshipper in order to get a wife. No," he added, " if I ever marry I must love the woman for what she is, not for what she possesses, nor for what advantage I might get by her." Then he resumes his work, and hums to himself the lines—

> Let fools for riches strive and toil,
> Let greedy minds divide the spoil,
>   It's all too mean for me.
> Above the earth, above the skies,
> My bold, my fervent wishes rise,
>   My God, to Heaven and Thee."

On settling in Dalkeith, James makes up his mind to attend the ministry of the Rev. Robert Buchanan, and he waits one day on the minister in order to give in his certificate. To his great delight he found him a most congenial, heavenly-minded man, but a bachelor, like his former minister at Wooler. Mr Buchanan at once shows his interest in the young man, and informs him that there is a library in connection with the church, and kindly adds that he may have free access to his own private one. He also invites him to give him as many of his spare evenings during the winter as he may find it convenient to do. James is filled with wonder and gratitude for God's goodness in giving him such an opportunity for self-improvement, and he gladly embraces it ; and during the following four winters he spends many happy and profitable hours with Mr Buchanan in the manse.

James also gets acquainted with a young brother of Janet's, who is also a saddler. They are not in the same workshop, but they often take long walks together in the summer evenings. They had both been brought up in the country, and after their long hours at work it was a great treat to them to breathe the country air. One evening about this time, James calls upon Willie to go for their evening walk, but he tells him that he is going down to the Bailie's to take out his sister, who has been feeling rather unwell, for a walk in the Duke's park.

"Go with me, and I will introduce you to her," says Willie. "Suppose I say it that maybe should not say it, she is a nice lassie, but her health has suffered a good deal through her long attendance and care over one of the Bailie's sick bairns."

"Willie," says James, "I never knew you had a sister in the Bailie's."

"No, I daresay, nor anybody else; she has been seen so little out of doors, for the reason I have mentioned. Come away, though; it's possible ye may fancy her for a wife."

Janet is waiting for her brother at the gate, and is not a little astonished to see a young man with him. James is not less astonished to find in Willie's sister the young woman to whom he sold some sponges three years before, and whose image had haunted him ever since. The evening is calm and beautiful; they walk along the side of the river Esk; the golden rays of the setting sun piercing through the woods make every tree look like a burning bush. James's frank manner, his intelligence, his knowledge of astronomy, as he describes the planets and stars which are now appearing, and speaks of their magnitudes, all captivate Janet. "What a glorious Being," he says, "must the Maker be, and yet this glorious God is our Father: we are His children." James is not less pleased with Janet's natural grace.

All that followed from this second interview is gathered up on the 20th day of January, when we find Janet in her bridal dress, and in the circumstances we have described. In the drawing-room are assembled Mr and Mrs Scott-Moncrieff, James's old minister, the eight children, the servants of the family, and three female friends. A few of these had not yet seen the bridegroom, and all eyes are naturally turned towards him as the most interesting person in the group. Willie has the part to play of giving away his sister to his friend; and now those two hearts, that for some time have in the sight of God been one, are acknowledged so in the holy ordinance of marriage. They were congratulated by all present, and Janet's cup of happiness might seem to others to overflow, but her dear boy, whom she had so tenderly nursed for years, is standing by his mamma's side weeping, and giving vent to his feelings in subdued sobs of grief. When Janet kisses him, and bids him and the family who had shown her so much kindness good-bye, she realises in her spirit how true it is that "there is no rose without a thorn."

We will follow the couple to their new home in

the outskirts of the town. They occupy the upper flat of a newly renovated house, the few apartments in which are well and neatly furnished, in keeping with their station in life. Janet had received many valuable and useful presents, not only from the family and her fellow-servants, but also from many of the family's relations; and all these helped to give even an air of elegance to their humble dwelling.

It will be expected that the regulations of the household will be such as becometh godliness, and at the outset they make a few rules which they purpose strictly to observe. They resolve, first, that they will have family worship night and morning; that they will be regular in their attendance on public worship; they will have no visiting or receiving of visitors on Sabbath, unless for mutual exhortation and prayer; no whisky or strong drink of any kind is to be used by them, unless in cases of illness; and they will have no formal tea parties, but always show kind hospitality to all who visit them. Then they fall on their knees and ask God to strengthen them, and help them to follow Him through evil report and good report; and they resolve that, setting the Lord always before them, they will not fear the face of man.

There was no total abstinence society in those days, and people were counted " mean " who did not keep a bottle for the entertainment of friends and visitors, especially when newly married. They had often to meet a charge of this kind, but it did not affect their resolution. When taunted with " meanness " for not keeping a bottle, James used to say he had observed, when he was very young, that, how-ever plain the food was, there was always thanks given, but he never yet saw thanks given for whisky. So he concluded that the person or persons partaking of it had at least a conscious feeling that it was not food, and was not a needful thing. His motto was, " Temperance in everything lawful and good."

As already stated, Janet's health had not been good for some time, and although she was now feel-ing considerably better, she was yet far from being strong. She was, however, by nature of a joyous spirit, and she often wondered at the goodness of God in giving her so many comforts and blessings. One day she said, " Oh, James, I never hoped to be so happy in this world as I am now."

James looks up somewhat sadly to her pale face, and says, " My dearest, let us rejoice with trembling, for the married state has its crosses and sorrows as well as its comforts and joys. We sail on a troubled and tempestuous sea, and we cannot but meet with a storm before we come to the end of our voyage. Let us therefore look to God to support us under heavy burdens, and sanctify our afflictions, as well as our comforts, for our spiritual good."

For three years Janet continued in poor health. She suffered much from a sore cough and shortness of breathing ; she had also had influenza fever, which left her very weak. Afterwards she had smallpox, and none who saw her suffering under this awful disease ever expected her recovery. One evening, one of her late fellow-servants called to ask for her, and seeing James sitting by her sick-bed, said to

him, " James, you have had little comfort in your
married life."

" Oh, Jenny," he replied, " you are greatly mis-
taken; all our afflictions have but led us nearer to
God, and closer to each other.   He afflicts not willingly, but for our profit ; therefore we can trust
him, believing He can make no mistakes.   Is not
this our gain and comfort ? "

Janet has now entered on the fourth year of her
married life.   After recovering from smallpox, she
had regained a measure of good health.   The bloom
has again returned to her cheek, and her step is
firmer than it had been for years.   Oh, the joy and
thankfulness that filled the hearts of husband and
wife, as everything appeared to prosper with them.
Their income was not great, but they were content.
The old foreman was still in the shop, but though he
retained the name James performed the duties ; and
when it was pointed out to him by a friend that if
he did the foreman's work he ought to get corres-
ponding wages, he said—" I may not myself live to
an old age, but no one will have it to say of me that
I behaved unkindly to an old man.   If in the
providence of God a better situation turns up, I am
free to take it ; still I will find it not only my duty
but my privilege to rise up before the hoary head
and honour the face of the old man."

His employer, seeing his unselfish spirit, and
wishing to remunerate him in some way, told James
that a house which he owned and had himself once
occupied, and which he thought would suit him, was
to be vacant shortly, and he purposed to let him

have it rent free. Janet's heart is lifted up. No rent! she could scarcely believe it. They had never been behind with the rent, nor other matters; and though their income was only fifteen shillings a week she had saved a few pounds. What will she save when she has no rent to pay! Besides, what a fine house! There is a main door, with a brass knocker, and the rooms are all oil-painted. She will buy a new carpet and sew a new rug, to be in keeping with the house. Then it will be so much nearer the shop, and her husband will get his meals more regularly. Having caught a cold in the early spring James had not been looking so well as before, and had a troublesome cough. But when they get to their new house in the town, she will be able to get little luxuries for him, and he will soon be well and strong. Thus she fondly reasoned and planned. She herself had been troubled with a cough for years, but now she felt much better. Oh, if they were into their new house, they would soon be well; and oh, how happy! Ah, Janet! hast thou turned a deaf ear to the voice that has followed thee all thy life, and which is continually whispering to thee, "Boast not thyself of to-morrow, for thou knowest not what a day may bring forth?"

James was greatly pleased with the prospect of improved circumstances and increased temporal comforts. For this he had long hoped, but he was somewhat surprised to see Janet so uplifted, as she had always been quite contented with their lot. One day he said—"My dear, one would think that since you heard of the new house you had forgotten John

Bunyan's motto—'He that is down need fear no fall, he that is low no pride, and he that is humble will ever have God to be his guide.' Let us not forget that it is not only said, 'In the day of prosperity be joyful,' but also, 'In the day of adversity consider.'"

Janet goes on making preparations for removing to their new home, but James's cough still continues, and he is daily losing strength. That year the winter set in very early, and was a long and stormy one. In November there was a heavy snowstorm, and it was thought advisable, while the storm lasted, that James should go to the shop only for a few hours each day, in order to see that the work was being duly attended to. But it turns out that, as the hours of labour are fewer, the wages are also ess. Janet has to draw upon her savings, in order to get cordials and other things necessary for her loved one; and she cheers herself with the hope that by the time the storm has disappeared, her husband will be much better. Then the fine spring weather will revive him, and the new house, and no rent, will soon make up for the present loss.

XXIII.

Passing through Deep Waters.

ANET had not hitherto come in contact with any one suffering from lung disease, but James, being a few years older, had seen more. He was beginning to doubt his own recovery, and to wonder how he could prepare her for the issue he apprehended. In some things ignorance may be bliss; but he thinks it right to give her a gentle hint as to his doubts and fears.

One night about this time there was a furious hurricane. Janet is busy making the new rug, and is entertaining James by telling him the story of how the wind blew the roof off the old house at Hartleap, and how it resulted in a new one being built. She adds, that they will forget all their troubles when they get into their new house. He listened for a while, and then, with a tone of gravity, which somewhat startled her, he said, " Janet, I did not ask a new house from God; and many a time while at work, when I have heard my master swearing and taking the holy name of God in vain, I have lifted up my heart in prayer that He would open up the

way for me to another situation, and cast my lot
where I would not have to hear His holy name
blasphemed. I believe that all true prayer is heard
and answered, but God, in His wisdom and knowledge of our need, often answers us in a way we do
not think of; and if He should see fit to answer my
prayer by sending His angels to carry me to Abraham's bosom, I would have no cause to complain."

For a moment his young wife is stunned, and con-
fusing thoughts rush through her mind. Does he
think that he is dying? Oh, surely no; perhaps it
is only a feeling of sadness, because he is off work.
He looks ill only when the cough troubles him; at
times he is cheerful, and takes his food well. She
will lay aside the rug, and read aloud for a while to
divert his mind from himself.

" Shall I read you," she says, " a little of John
Knox's ' History of the Reformation ' or a bit from
' Brainerd's Life,' or some other good book ? "

" My dear," he replied, " I have lost all taste for
such books; I find more help to my spirit in the
Gospel of St John than in all the books I possess or
ever read. I have seen there that many of our ideas
are wrong as regards the work of Christ; I have come
to see that Christ did not purchase the love of the
Father, as I had thought, but that He came to reveal
it. How we have misunderstood the meaning of the
words Christ spoke—' God so loved the world that
He *gave* His only begotten Son, that whosoever be-
lieveth in Him should have everlasting life.' I am
just beginning to see the glory of God in the face of
Jesus Christ as I have not seen it before, and to

understand how it is that to know God, and Jesus Christ whom He has sent, is eternal life."

While James was thus confined to the house, several young men, seeking after self-improvement, used to look in occasionally to converse with him on various subjects, and in these conversations he took much interest. A visit from his minister was also a source of great delight to him. One day a gentleman, to whom, in his days of health, he had rendered a special service, called to ask for him. This man was of a kindly disposition, but had the habit, which was common then, as it is still, of taking God's name in vain. Every time he did so, James lifted the cap, which he wore in the house, from his head, saying, " Sir, I have a reverence for the name of my God." After he had left, James remarked, " I have not sat with vain persons, neither have I gone in with dissemblers. God will not gather my soul with sinners, nor my life with wicked men."

The winter was now far advanced ; the weather had been severely cold, and James had faded like a leaf, till Janet is beginning to fear the worst. She prays that, if it be the will of God to take him away, He will deal gently with him ; will remove the fear of death, and give him a place among the pure and the holy ; and that He will be pleased to give her strength of body and calmness of spirit to wait on him to the end. She wept as well as prayed, but she did so in secret, for she would not add to her loved one's distress by showing her grief. James was too quick of discernment, however, not to perceive her sorrow; and one day he called her to him and said, "My dear, you have been weeping."

"I have," she said, "for, Oh, my dear James, I have begun to fear that you are dying."

"Be it so, my love," he meekly replied; "do we not know that if our earthly house of this tabernacle were dissolved, we have a building of God, a house not made with hands, eternal in the heavens? Our heavenly Father is seeking by these afflictions to purify us, and make us meet to sit down at the marriage supper of the Lamb. Then we shall look on death as one of the things of the past, and spend a long eternity together. But, in saying so, I do not say, weep not; it would be unnatural not to weep. Human love is very sweet, but Divine love is infinitely better. Oh, lift your tearful eyes above; truly you have a friend in God, and God is love."

The ice is now broken, the flood-gates are burst open, the waters overflow their banks, and, husband and wife, each finds a great relief. They have opened their minds to each other, so that they can now converse calmly and freely on the things that belong to their temporal and eternal wellbeing.

The fourth anniversary of their wedding day has come round. They bless God for sparing them so long together, and ask for strength and help to hallow their heavenly Father's name, and that His will may be done in the inner chambers of their hearts, so that, whether in life or in death, they may be ever with the Lord. But another burden lies heavy on Janet's heart, and her sick one is too weak to share its weight. He must not know, for it would overwhelm him. Her little savings are nearly exhausted; she must try to earn something. But what can she do? She must not go out of the house whilst he has to be attended to. She is now afraid that he may not get better, but he has not as yet been confined to bed. If only he should be spared, though it were but to sit beside her, how willingly she would work so as to get all he needed. She has still a half-crown, besides some articles of food and a little coal. That is nearly used up, it is true; but God will open up her way. If spared till to-morrow, she will run out for a few minutes and see what she can get in the way of washing.

The morrow brings new wants, which have to be supplied, and when the purchases are made Janet finds that only a shilling is left in her hands. She will go out in the afternoon to see about the washing. When the little quantity of soup she had been preparing is ready, she says cheerily, "Now, dear, I have made it a little earlier, as you were sooner up this morning, and it will strengthen you."

So saying, she set forward the small table. After giving thanks, James tried to lift the spoon. She thought he looked as if he did not care for the soup, and said, "Perhaps you would have liked something else?"

"Oh no, dear Janet, it looks very fine; but I feel the spoon heavy to-day. Will you help me with it?"

The words came as a surprise, and, like an arrow shot from an unexpected quarter, deeply wounded her spirit, as with aching heart and trembling hand she assisted him in taking a little of the soup. He appeared to relish it, and, as Janet fondly thought, was strengthened by it. Then he rose from his seat and walked across the floor. After standing a few moments at the window he remarked that it was surely a very cloudy day. Janet says, "Oh, James, the sun is shining brightly; it is a lovely day!"

"Alas! I fear then that the mists of death are coming over me. Come near me, my dear, and let me lean on your shoulder. I must go to bed.

After being laid down, he said, "Don't leave me; come near, and let me kiss your lips once more. Of all the unnumbered blessings which God has graciously bestowed on me, and of which I have been unworthy, you have not been the least—a true, loving wife. Janet, you have been to me all that I could desire, not only as a wife, but you have given me all the affectionate care of a mother. I have had a great struggle to give you up, but God has given me the victory. You are no more mine; I give you back into His hands from whom I received you. You are young, and I have feared exceedingly the temptations you may be exposed to. May a curse fall on any one who would harm a hair of your head, and may the blessing of the God of Jacob rest on him that may protect you! Never forsake God, and He will never forsake you." Then he added, "There is another thing that lies heavy on my heart; since my mother's death I have seen in my brothers and sisters a great backsliding, and I have not been faithful in warning them to flee from the wrath to come. I ask this favour of you—to try and see them, and tell them my dying regrets. Tell them to prepare for death, for it is a solemn thing to die. Now I have no more to say ; only, my dear, lay your soft hand in mine, and let us pray."

He feebly tried to raise his other hand, then lifted his eyes up to heaven, and with a tremulous voice said, "Lord Jesus, into Thy hands I commit my sinful soul ; O receive it to Thyself, and present it in Thy Father's presence without spot or wrinkle. Amen." There was one mild look, one gentle groan, one long, long sigh, and life had fled.

The clock had just struck two on this 5th of February, 1836. But where can words be found to express, or pen to write, the anguish of that young widow's heart. She is stunned. She wildly utters, —"Oh, is it true ? Is it not a dream ? Surely he cannot be dead ! "

Then she tries to raise him in the bed, but the head falls back as she folds the lifeless body in her arms. She lays herself down to die—she cannot live—all is whirl and confusion—everything around her seems to be like dust blowing from a road on a windy day. She cannot weep, she cannot pray. Oh, for one tear to ease her bursting heart ! But that will not come ; she is like a withered tree whose sap is all dried up.

How long she thus lay, stricken and desolate, she could never tell ; but sometime afterwards a rap came to the door, and the minister, accompanied by her brother Robert, entered. She took no notice of the kind salutation of the man of God, but stared with a strange bewildered look, and in a trembling voice, said, " Sir, is he happy ? Is he safe ? Oh, tell me, is he home, home to the Father's house? Has his soul escaped like a bird from a snare?"

Mr Buchanan was amazed, but collecting himself, he said, "Mrs Kemp, what is wrong?" Then his eye caught a sight of all that remained of his friend, and he looked round and said, "How is this? Why are you alone?"

Janet took no notice of what he said, but in her wild agony still kept inquiring eagerly, "Tell me, tell me, is he safe?"

"Mrs Kemp," said the minister, "your husband was no ordinary man. For one in his station of life, for Christian deportment and intelligence, I have not met his equal. From what I have known of him, I could this moment risk my own soul in his soul's stead."

Her brother had thrown himself upon the bed, and was bewailing bitterly the loss of him who was truly a brother beloved. The little sorrowing company then bowed the knee, and the minister leads their prayers. God pities the chief mourner. A calm and heavenly breeze passes over her heated brow; and she finds that whatever she has lost, God still remains.

> Prayer is the breath of God in man,
>   Ascending from whence it came.
> Love is the fire that burns within,
>   And prayer's the rising flame.
>
> When God inclines the heart to pray
>   He has an ear to hear.
> To Him there's music in a groan,
>   And beauty in a tear.

XXIV.

He is Faithful that Promised.

POOR Janet! this 5th of February afternoon has work for her of a more
solemn kind than looking out for
washing. The thunder cloud has
burst with tremendous force, and has
washed out of her heart the vain thoughts of a
new house and saving money. She knows that
God is behind the cloud, but still it is very dark.
Funeral expenses and the rent of the present house
face her and her one shilling, but she will look
up to her Father in Heaven, who is very pitiful.
She retires to her closet to tell Him all her woe,
and falls on her knees, but not a word can she
utter. He that used to be the burden of her pleading
is beyond her reach, and needs it no more. As for
herself, what is life to her now? The first prayer
taught at her mother's knee—" Our Father "—rises
to her lips, not now merely in words, but from the
deep pit of a grief-stricken heart ; and there comes a
peace more calm than the summer breeze, more refreshing than the morning dew, and a voice saying,
" Woman, why weepest thou? Thy loved one is not
lost. He has only entered another chamber of the

heavenly house above, gone into the immediate presence of the eternal Friend whose name is Love."

The load in some measure is removed from her, and, like Thomas, she says, "My Lord and my God,

> Though death my James and me divide,
> Thou dost not, Lord, my sorrows chide,
>   Nor frown my tears to see.
> Restrained from passionate excess,
> I calmly mourn in deep distress
>   For him that followed Thee."

The funeral is over. Brother Willie settles with the grave-digger, but the coffin has yet to be paid for. For that the bereaved one must work, but it will be long ere she can make up the sum required. The one shilling is long since spent, and the little stock of provisions is almost exhausted. Janet's father had died during the previous summer, and she had then got mourning apparel, which has been very little worn. Neatly dressed in her widow's weeds, with her house tidy and clean, no one appeared to see any sign of poverty, or think of her empty purse and her bare pantry. She takes in sewing, and resolves that she will live on one meal in the day till she gets the undertaker paid. But where is that one meal to come from before she finishes the six shirts she has in hand, and gets payment for them? She makes complaint to no one, but weeps and sews on, and prays and reminds God of His promise that " bread shall be given and water shall be sure." He who feedeth the ravens and the young lions has taken away her breadwinner; and whilst she is willing to labour, working at anything or in any way, she remembers that He is her shepherd, and believes that she shall not want.

But now Janet's whole stock is exhausted—not even a handful of meal nor a crust of bread remains. One very cold, rainy night the wind blew a very hurricane; the fire has gone out, for no coal is left; there is not a cinder nor a bit of stick with which to kindle a fire in the morning. She is feeling the pangs of hunger. But the house still stands, she has still a bed; many a one has not so much. In this stormy night she feels that it might have been worse with her, and she calmly commits herself to God. The storm continues until the morning; but, although the wind had abated, the rain still fell heavily. The room looked cold and cheerless, yet Janet must rise early and get on with her sewing. She thinks of the sailors and others who have been exposed to the hurricane's fury, and with a thankful heart she thanks God for His preserving care over her.

She sits down to her work at the window, which looks into one of the Duke's parks. Many of the trees are blown down; all about the little village was strewn with chimney cans, slates, and tiles; everything looked dismal in the rain; yet Janet remembered one of her mother's proverbs—"It's an ill wind that blows nobody good." Even here there may be good, although she cannot see it. Seven o'clock comes, and with it a gentle rap at her door; she is startled, and asks herself, what if some one has been killed? Oh, if it should be her brother! She hastened to open the door, and to her surprise there is Mr Corbet, the Duke's forester, who accosts her as follows—

"Good morning, Mrs Kemp; I am glad to find you up this cold, rainy morning. It is perhaps early enough to disturb you, but I have come to ask a great favour of you. In the first place, I may tell you that we have been greatly put about during the night. Part of our house has been blown down, and what remains is not safe. We have taken out all our furniture, and, notwithstanding all our endeavours to cover it up, the heavy rain is destroying everything. I have been running hither and thither trying to get a house to put it in, and have as yet been unsuccessful. At last it occurred to me that you might not be using all your apartments, and if you could make room for us to put in our best things in the meantime, it would greatly oblige us."

"Mr Corbet," said Janet, "I only occupy my bedroom; there is a small room on the stair-head, from which an old woman has lately removed; if you could send some of your men to remove my furniture into it, I shall gladly let you have the kitchen and sitting-room."

"God bless you, Mrs Kemp, for your readiness to oblige us in this day of our need. But why, may I ask, in this cold morning have you not your fire kindled?"

"Oh, well, I will have it kindled by-and-bye," she replied.

The good man appeared to guess the reason why

the fire was not kindled, and he immediately sent a man with a barrowful of dry logs to Janet's house. Mrs Corbet soon afterwards came over to see about moving the things, and noticing Janet's pale, cold-looking face, asked if she had not had breakfast. The reply was "Not yet;" and then Mrs Corbet went off and returned in a few minutes with a little jug of warm tea, and a roll of bread, toasted and buttered. One may judge the woman's feelings when Janet said, "Oh, thank you, Mrs Corbet; God has not only put it in your power, but also in your heart, to supply the need of a poor unworthy creature. I may tell you now that I have not tasted food for the last four-and-twenty hours."

Oh, it is sweet to be fed so directly from the hand of God. Never again will she doubt His goodness. How pleasant were the words of the children's hymn to her in that hour—

Poor and needy though I be, God Almighty cares for me:
Gives me clothing, shelter, food ; gives me all I have of good.
He who reigns above the sky, once was poorer far than I ;
He by whom the world was made, had not where to lay His
     head.
Jesus laid His glory by, when for me He stooped to die,
How I wonder when I see His unbounded love to me !

Every bird can build its nest, foxes have their place of rest ;
But He by whom the worlds were made had not where to lay
     His head !
Though I labour here awhile, He will bless me with His smile ;
And when this short life is past, He'll receive my soul at last.
Then to Him I'll tune my song, happy as the day is long ;
And this my joy shall ever be, God Almighty cares for me.

Mr Corbet called in the evening and told Janet that it was a part of his engagement that the Duke should give him a free house ; and that he had been calling on the factor, her old master, and had told him how ready she had been to oblige him. "I said," he continued, "that he ought to relieve you of this half-year's rent, which he readily consented to do. He also sends you this half-sovereign, and bids me tell you that Mrs Scott-Moncrieff wishes to see you."

Janet is filled with wonder, love, and praise. She has waited on God ; and, truly, her soul is not cast down. He is loading her with His benefits till she longs that all the world might taste and see the riches of His grace.

Janet visits her old mistress, and is received kindly. Mrs Scott-Moncrieff expresses her deep sympathy with her, and asks her in what way she is purposing to help herself. Janet tells her that, as her brother Robert is working in the Duke's gardens, she has thought, if she could get a small house near the gate, that he might get lodgings with her. He would give her six shillings a week for his board, and she would take in sewing. It would not take much, she says, to keep herself, though it might be a little difficult to make up the rent.

Mrs Scott-Moncrieff said, " I fear, Janet, that would be a very foolish step. Your brother would be bringing his companions about the house, and you might be led into great temptations. Listen to me. You are young, and a good servant ; I have no opening in my family at present, but my sister, Mrs

Christie, is in want of a maid for herself, and I know she would be delighted to have you. Your wages would be good, and you would have no care. My advice to you is, sell off your furniture, and she will receive you at once."

Janet's heart sank within her. She could easily see that from Mrs Scott-Moncrieff's point of view the thing looked feasible. She was sure that the advice was well meant, and in a worldly point of view it was the best thing she could do; but to her mind the sacrifice would be great, and the evil would overbalance the good. To have a home, however humble, her own quiet fireside, her morning and evening devotions, her quiet Sabbath, even with no more than a potato and salt, was a great possession. And how could she sell the furniture that cost her loved one so much self-sacrifice in order to provide for her comfort? how could she part with her beautiful chest of drawers—her mistress's gift to her on her marriage day—and all the other valuable presents she had received? To give up all these, and go into a large house amongst a retinue of servants, male and female, gay, thoughtless, and worldly— perhaps not a pious one amongst them—would be unbearable. She felt that she would be tenfold more exposed to temptation there than she could possibly be in her own home. The very thought of being ushered into such surroundings made her tremble; and, however unwilling she felt to displease one from whom she had received so much kindness, she was compelled positively to refuse her proposals.

Mrs Scott-Moncrieff could not understand Janet's

scruples. Indeed, she was displeased with her decision, and said that it was a principle on which she acted, to help people to help themselves. She had done her best, she said, to help her, but if she persisted in taking her own way she must hang by her own tether. Janet had expected sympathy—and she got it in the way her old mistress thought best—but she returned home with a heavy addition to her already great burden of grief. She could conceive of a day coming, and of circumstances occurring, when she might be compelled to sell all she had. This she would rather do than be in debt; but if she only had the funeral chest paid for she would never take on another halfpenny. She is hopeful that she will soon make up the sum she needs. She will save a little of the half sovereign, and will soon get in the money for her sewing.

The young men who used to visit James were well-disposed, intelligent youths—shop lads, two of them being tobacconists and two grocers. After her husband's death, they had come now and again to ask after Janet's health, and a few days after her interview with Mrs Scott-Moncrief they called, and told her that they had been consulting together, and that, though she had said nothing to them of her needs, they could not conceive how it was possible for her to have saved anything, seeing that she was so recently married and her husband had been so long off work. They had made up their minds each to contribute ten shillings, and they now begged her to do them the kindness to accept a present of two pounds; and in doing so they asked, as a particular favour, that she would tell no one, adding, " You are a young woman and we are young men, and a bad use might be made of what is only meant for good."

Janet knows that this gift comes to her because of the high respect they had for the dear departed, and she expresses her gratitude in a flood of tears.

After they had left, she said to herself, " Oh, what is this ? Where I expected a little help, I got none ; where I could least expect it, I have got much. Is there anything too hard for God ? My every want is supplied, my debt is paid, and yet my purse is not empty nor my pantry bare."

It is now the middle of May ; Janet has removed to the back street of the town into a house of two apartments, a goodly-sized kitchen and a room opening off it, in which her brother Robert is comfortably lodged. She is taking in white seam sewing, but is sometimes troubled at being most of the day alone. Then she has time to think and weep ; and, in spite of herself, her work is often soiled with tears. But she labours on, giving God thanks for the many mercies vouchsafed to her. Her brother conducts family worship, and they go to the house of God in company. Their Sabbaths are days of peaceful rest. She has her own fireside. There is no want of a closet where she can shut her door and pray to her Father in Heaven, who seeth in secret, but rewardeth openly. She has food and raiment, and is therewith content.

Miss M'Murdie, a good Christian lady who had visited her after her husband's death, one day called to see her in her new abode. It was afternoon ; the house was in good order, and everything had the appearance of comfort ; but Janet's slender form, her pale face, and tearful eyes drew pity from the heart of this Christian woman. She said,

" Mrs Kemp, you are too much alone, I fear ; I think if you were to get two or three little girls and teach them to sew, and give them lessons, you might do them good, and it would help to divert your thoughts from yourself. Your indulging in unavailing grief is neither glorifying to God nor good for yourself."

" Oh, dear ma'am," said Janet, " you are very kind, and I am thankful for your consideration, but I must tell you I am not a learned woman. I never was six weeks at a regular school at one time, and I feel that it would be the very height of presumption for me to pretend or attempt to teach any one."

" But, listen to me, Mrs Kemp : you can read your Bible, and if you can teach one or two little girls to do so, and set a good example before them, you will not have lived in vain. You also sew neatly, and I am certain that many a mother would be glad to have her little girls under your training. Just you let it be known that you purpose taking in a few little girls to teach them to sew and to read little lessons ; let them bring each a little stool with them, so that you can pack them under your kitchen bed in the evening, and have your kitchen clear when your brother comes in at night. Now think over it, commit it to God, and He will open up your way."

" That is just what I would like," says Janet, " but I feel it presumption to try. I would be ashamed to make the thing known. Nevertheless, many thanks, dear ma'am. I will think over what you have said."

After the lady left, Janet considered the proposal, but the more she thought it over, the more absurd it appeared. What would Mrs Scott-Moncrieff think? She knew how ignorant she was; and she would laugh when she remembered her first letter and the green map.

Shortly after Miss M'Murdie left, an old neighbour called to ask for Janet. She relates to her what had just been suggested. The woman thinks the thing very feasible, and when she returns home to Lugton, the little village from which Janet had removed, she makes known among her neighbours what she is likely to do. The news spreads, and the following Monday there came a rap at the door. The visitor was a little girl who used to go messages for Janet during her husband's illness. Now she was carrying a little stool, and had with her a book, and cloth to be made into an apron for her mother, and twopence in her hand, which she presented to Janet, saying, " I am come to your school, and this is my school wages."

" My dear little Barbara Bell, I have not a school," was the reply ; " but come in."

Janet's heart was moved to see the disappointment of the little girl, and she made up her mind to take her in for the week, thinking she would tell Barbara on Saturday not to come back till she sent for her. Poor Janet! God is doing that for her which she could not do for herself, and ere the end of the week she has nine scholars, and is beginning to feel as if the thing was of God. She knew that it was written that He "hath chosen the weak things of the world to confound the things which are mighty;" and though she feels weak and ignorant, as she has done hitherto, she will set the Lord always before her and follow where He leads. Then she thinks how delightful it will be to tell those little lambs all about the Good Shepherd. She will draw out a plan by which she will be guided, asking God to help her, and she will thus arrange her little school on the Monday following.

Monday morning comes, and she is all in readiness to receive her little flock. She remembers how the little lambs at Summerhope used to follow her, and how often she wished that she could teach them to reverence the Sabbath. God has now given her some of His own lambs, and she will tell them how good He is, even permitting them when they pray to say, "Our Father which art in Heaven." It is ten o'clock, the school door is opened; and to her surprise, instead of nine, she has eighteen scholars, including two little boys, each carrying a little stool and twopence for school wages. She takes down their names and arranges them as well as she can. Then she tells them that God made and keeps them every one by His great power, that He loves them, that when wicked men mocked Jesus, God's beloved Son, then children sang His praise; and He was pleased, and took them in his arms and blessed them. Then they stand and lift up their eyes and hearts to Heaven, and praise His holy name by singing a part of the eighth Psalm. Janet leads, and they all join in as best they can, and then there is a short prayer. Thus following in the footsteps of the Good Shepherd, she goes before her little flock, and they follow. How many of them will be found in the heavenly fold eternity will declare.

Janet's school prospers, and the parents get a blessing through the children. Mrs Scott-Moncrieff hears of Janet's success in her new sphere; she visits her, and is amazed; the good manners and intelligence of the children surprise her. She still wished to be helpful to her, and asked her to come an hour every day, after she dismissed the school, to give her two younger children, Joanna and John, a lesson. In this Janet felt that she could be of little use to Mrs Scott-Moncrieff's children. She herself always gave her children their first lessons. But Janet saw in this the wisdom, as well as the kindness of her old mistress. No doubt she considered that this step would give Janet a higher standing in the public mind, and also prepare the way for a larger field of usefulness. Janet had loved her mistress from the day she knew her, and ever felt indebted to her for her Christian example and motherly care.

Janet is filled with wonder at the wisdom and goodness of God, by which all her earthly wants are supplied. Now she has six shillings a week for her brother's board, the fees from her eighteen scholars, and a sum from Mrs Scott-Moncrieff; and though she has her hands full, she is gathering strength of body, her soul is feasting on the fat things of God's own house, her heart is eased, and her eyes enlightened.

Having followed Janet thus far through her career, we feel constrained to take our leave of her—not because her journey is ended or her further history is less interesting, but because the aim of the writer is not to make her the object of interest, but to lead those who may read this story to put their trust in God.   He is faithful to all His promises.   He faileth not, neither is weary.   He is long-suffering and slow to wrath, abundant in goodness and truth.   He is not willing that any should perish, but that all should have eternal life.   If her nieces, while reading this tale of her humble life, have their eyes opened to see the leadings of an unseen Fatherly hand, and if their faith is strengthened to follow in Aunt Janet's footsteps, in so far as she has followed Christ, they will find that she has left them a legacy of far more value than silver and gold or houses and lands.

The Widow's Consolation.

AH, who hath marked the silent flow
   Of secret tears, that flood of woe,
The sob suppressed, the bloodless cheek,
The step so firm, but oh! so weak;
And seen not in the 'wildered eye
The burning mark of agony?

There was an hour, but that hour has gone,
A day when that mourner did not mourn,
When her cup was full till its brim was laved,
And the wildest of earth's wild joys uncraved,
For prosperity mixed, at her feet was thrown
The stores of a heart she could call her own.

But a moment has come—nay, it was an age,
Which blotted the whole from her life's first page;
For the shadow went back to her childhood's years,
And bathed the evening of life in tears;
But it fell with the speed of the whirlwind's blast,
It breathed on her love, and he breathed his last.

There was one mild look, one gentle groan,
One long, long sigh, and the life was gone!
And now she is in the world alone—
There are thousands around, but her own is gone.
How her heart grows cold at the thought of life,
As the widow creeps in on the name of wife.

And strange dark thoughts of the peaceful tomb
Suggest for the moment a self-made home—
But such thoughts depart, as the muddy flow
Of the new born fountain's first infant throe,
When the sparkling liquid has washed its lips,
Till their surface is pure as the water it sips.

So sweet deep streams that are buried there,
Come up from the heart while engaged in prayer ;
And tears, sweet tears—that blessed relief,
Whose anointing is healing for inward grief,
The calm repose, the placid fear,
And the heartfelt reliance that God is near.

While rising she feels in her moments of need,
There's a Husband for those that are widows indeed.
She asks to be led in the path that her Saviour trod,
She looks on her dead, and leans on her God.

On Revisiting the Scene of my Childhood.

FULL seventy years of weary toil
　　And ups and downs I'd borne,
I came back to the pleasant vale
　　I left in life's fair morn.

Up I got and took the road
　　One bonnie summer day,
To view the place my feet had trod
　　When life was young and gay.

Alang the haugh, across the brig—
　　Ilk step it seemed a mile,
Until I reached the boontree bush
　　And there sat down awhile.

O Philiphaugh ! my early hame,
　　In Ettrick's lonely vale,
How changed is now thy hamely face
　　Since last I did thee hail.

Threescore and ten years have gane o'er
　　My weary head this day,
The chestnut locks that graced my neck
　　Are changed to silver grey.

I turned up the weel kenned road
    That led me to our hame ;
Transfixed with wonder there I stood,
    For every house had gane.

With modern grandeur they have built,
    Ravensheugh, by name,
They've ploughed where yince the auld anes stood,
    They have'na left a stane.

They've fenced it here, they've fenced it there,
    They've ploughed baith east and west,
They've scarcely left a heather bush
    For birds to build their nest.

I ran to ilka weel ken'd nook,
    Like one that was insane,
And tears came coursing o'er my cheeks
    Like heavy drops o' rain.

I sought the tree beneath whose shade
    We bairns played mony a game,
And filled our laps wi' Scots fir taps
    Before we scampered hame.

I view'd the hill which oft I'd climbed,
    How oft I canna tell,
And chased the muirfowl frae its nest,
    And pu'ed the heather bell.

O happy day! can I forget ?
    Far, far frae strife and din,
My brother John did tend his flock
    Close by the Corbie Linn.

And when his hamely meal I brang
    And shared the sport wi' him,
O gumpin' mennens in the brook—
    It's all now like a dream.

Oh me! my heart is sair,
  Muckle waur it canna be;
Yonder at Tibbie Tamson's grave
  I could lie doon and dee.

Sair grieved, I sought the wee spring well
  Amang the rashes green,
And sat yince mair upon the seat
  I oft had sat lang syne.

'Twas there I watched the purlin' brook
  Take mony a sportin' turn,
'Twas there I pu'ed the buttercups
  That grew beside the burn.

'Twas there I filled my wee brown can
  Wi' water fresh and clear,
To cool the burning thirst of one
  Whose death was drawing near.

Spring up, thou little well, spring up,
  There is no change in thee;
Thy pure, cool waters bubblin' up
  These threescore years and three.

How lang before I canna tell,
  How lang ye yet may be;
O could my stammering tongue but tell
  Half I've been taught by thee.

Spring up, thou little well, spring up,
  Thy waters pure and free;
No emblem more sublime suggests
  A Saviour's love to me.

Boil up, you little well, boil up,
  Your basin may rin toom,
But o' the spring my soul doth drink
  The fountain is aboon.

For He that sat by Jacob's well
　This day hath met wi' me,
And led me to the fountain-head —
　A Father's love to see.

O the Eternal Father's love,
　O overflowing tide!
He sent His well beloved Son
　To earth to woo His Bride.

He found her all polluted
　In sorrow, shame, and sin;
He passed through death to save her,
　And make her pure within.

He threw His arms around her,
　Put diamond on her brow,
And He walks and lives beside her,
　An everlasting now.

O the glory!　O the glory!
　Of God's eternal Son,
The Brother of Humanity,
　He victory hath won.

O speak ye forth His praises!
　Ye rivers and ye rills,
And echo back the story,
　Ye heather-covered hills.

O clap your hands, ye lofty trees,
　O feathered family, sing;
For He is our Creator,
　Our rightful Lord and King.

Dear Lord, my heart is sick of love,
　Here would I like to dwell,
And hold communion with Thee
　Beside this little well.

But Thou hast further work for me,
  I've other nooks to see;
Dear Lord, do Thou go with me
  And aye abide with me.

Farewell, thou little bubbling well,
  Thy face I'll nae mair see;
May other weary pilgrims learn
  The lessons thou'st taught me!

Again I sought the weel ken'd spot
  Where stood my father's hame,
And thought on a' the dear loved friends—
  Alas! where are they gane?

Where are dear mother's circling arms,
  That round my neck did twine?
And where the happy faces now
  That shared her heart wi' mine?

Speak, O ye proud and lofty trees,
  Do speak and let me know;
They shook their branches in my face,
  And seemed to mock my woe.

The happy vision cometh back:
  A father's reverend air,
A priest upon his throne, he sat
  In the old high-back'd chair.

And when the evening shadows fell,
  And labour all was o'er,
He brought the big auld Bible down
  And mother locked the door.

Then with a father's kindly smile,
  And an approving nod,
"Now bairns, compose yoursel's," he'd say,
  "And let us worship God."

O had they let the auld wa's stand,
  They might have had a tongue,
And echoed back the prayers and psalms
  That oft therein were sung.

But I sat upon the cauld green sward
  Where lay our auld hearth stane,
Where first upon my mother's lap
  I lisped Jehovah's name.

Now she is gane, but He remains
  The true and faithful One,
And on His arm I mean to lean
  Till travelling days are done.

Farewell, dear Philiphaugh, farewell!
  You've nae joy now for me;
A lonely widow, I maun sit
  Close by yon old elm tree.

I looked around, then turned away
  Frae that place once so dear,
And crossed the little rippling burn
  And o'er it shed a tear.

Then dander'd hame to sit my lane
  And think on what I'd seen,
Till kindly sleep did o'er me creep
  And closed my weary een.

JANET BATHGATE.

PRINTED BY GEORGE LEWIS AND SON, SELKIRK.

www.ingramcontent.com/pod-product-compliance
Lightning Source LLC
Chambersburg PA
CBHW081257110426
42743CB00045B/3181